TVA AND THE POWER FIGHT, 1933-1939

CRITICAL PERIODS  OF HISTORY

Robert D. Cross AND *Paul K. Conkin,*
GENERAL EDITORS

TVA AND THE POWER FIGHT

1933-1939

by
THOMAS K. McCRAW
University of Texas

J.B. LIPPINCOTT COMPANY
Philadelphia ☐ New York ☐ Toronto

In memory of Carey

PREFACE

"... In the minds of men the world over, the initials TVA stand for progress...." President John F. Kennedy, May 18, 1963.

"By God, if ever we could do it, before we leave here, I'd like to see us <u>sell</u> the whole thing, but I suppose we can't go that far." President Dwight D. Eisenhower, July 31, 1957.[1]

THE TENNESSEE VALLEY AUTHORITY generates more electricity and burns more coal than any other agency in the United States, public or private. It does many other things too. It controls floods, develops inland waterways, studies the Valley economy, builds parks, and produces new fertilizers. But none of these functions accounts for the TVA's harshly controversial history—explains why its birth was so belated and painful, why it received so much legal and verbal attack in the 1930s, why it still evokes strong emotions pro and con. The reason for these things is that TVA is in the electric power business, and its rates to consumers are extremely low.

The power industry, in net capital investment America's largest, grew from two mutually hostile traditions: a private tradition, which started it and built most of its network of generators and high-tension lines; and a public tradition, which tried to curb private financial and political excesses, sometimes by going into the business itself. On a collision course since the turn of the twentieth century, the two traditions met head-on when Franklin D. Roosevelt entered the White House in 1933.

FDR's New Deal, initially popular with many businessmen, won no affection from utility magnates, who reacted violently to such measures as the Tennessee Valley Authority Act. Roosevelt's assignment to the TVA of "yardstick" functions made the ensuing struggle one of the bitterest fights between business and government of the 1930s or any other decade. On the public side the standard bearer was TVA's brilliant young director David E. Lilienthal, and on the private the equally able Wendell L. Willkie of Commonwealth and Southern Corporation. Both men were destined for national prominence after the New Deal as well as during it. As they fought each other, both had to contend with trouble behind their own lines—Lilienthal with TVA's board chairman, the profound but eccentric Arthur E. Morgan, Willkie with moss-backed utility executives whose reluctance to acknowledge the public's stakes in their business invited still more interference by the government. Though TVA won the immediate battle, Willkie's losing performance earned him major public applause. A rapid rise to political glory followed, and in the presidential election of 1940 he took on not one of FDR's lieutenants but "the champ" himself.

If there was a Power Trust the New Deal tamed it. And though the industry differs fundamentally from most others, the utility fight suggests the major virtues and limits of New Deal economic reform. Roosevelt's approach to the power question, more consistent than most of his policies, still lacked intellectual coherence. The result was needless confusion not only for the men in charge of a vital industry, but for some dedicated public officials, who spent endless hours arguing among themselves about what FDR really wanted.

I acquired heavy obligations in writing this book. My wife, Susan M. McCraw, edited every page and helped organize three chapters. From start to finish Professor Paul W. Glad of the University of Wisconsin assisted me in many different ways, not least by serving as an exemplary scholar and teacher. Two participants in the story read the entire manuscript and made many helpful suggestions: James C. Bonbright, former professor of finance at Columbia University; and Chairman Joseph C. Swidler of the New York Public Service Commission, who served TVA for twenty-four years. The editor of this series, Professor Paul K. Conkin of the University of Wisconsin, pointed out dozens of small ways to improve the manuscript and discussed the TVA and the New Deal with me periodically for two years. None of these persons bears any responsibility for my errors.

Of the many TVA employees who helped me, I owe most to my father, John C. McCraw, a TVA engineer since 1933; Helen Watson, who patiently guided me through the Administrative Files; and Chief Librarian Jesse Mills, who accommodates researchers in the superb manner characteristic of his predecessor, Bernard L. Foy. Professor Charles W. Crawford of Memphis State University facilitated my research in his admirable TVA oral history project. The librarians and archivists of the Franklin D. Roosevelt Library, the Edison Electric Institute, Antioch College, the Library of Congress, the National Archives, the University of Tennessee, the Memphis Public Library, and Princeton University were all of great assistance.

THOMAS K. McCRAW

Austin, Texas
November, 1970

CONTENTS

1

THE PUBLIC AND PRIVATE TRADITIONS

BEFORE IT EMPTIES INTO the Ohio at Paducah, Kentucky, the Tennessee River drains 40,000 square miles in seven states, mostly Tennessee and Alabama. In the 37 miles of rapids called Muscle Shoals, in northern Alabama, the river drops 134 feet, creating an enormous water power potential and a severe impediment to navigation. During the nineteenth century public attention frequently focused on the rapids as a barrier to river traffic, but repeated attempts to build canals around them all ended more or less in failure. Only a dam, which would flood the shoals, would end the navigation problem. But dams cost huge sums of money, and the potential saving to shippers could not begin to justify a dam at Muscle Shoals.

World War I gave the shoals new importance. Preparedness legislation of 1916 authorized the president to construct nitrate plants for munitions, and a hydroelectric dam to supply the plants with power. Completed in 1925, it was named Wilson Dam for the late president whose administration had selected the site. At the time it was one of the largest concrete structures in the world.

After Armistice Day, the two nitrate plants and the unfinished dam appeared to be expensive white elephants. And the presence of government structures capable of producing vendible items such as electricity and nitrate fertilizer offended

the Harding administration's sensibilities about government
in business. Accordingly, Harding and the two Republican
presidents who followed him strove to sell or lease the project
to private entrepreneurs. But this solution, successfully applied to many other war plants, did not work with Muscle
Shoals. No satisfactory private bid came forth. And a small,
dedicated group of legislators worked tirelessly to keep the
project in the public domain. Thus Muscle Shoals became a
political football, one of the most durable and monotonous
questions before Congress in the 1920s. No subject except
prohibition elicited more rhetoric and passion, more proposals and counterproposals. For one thing, fertilizer was
part of the persistent farm problem. For another, Muscle
Shoals meant electricity, an issue affecting farmers and everyone else too.

To the first generation of the twentieth century, electric
power represented the potential key to a new kind of civiliza-
tion. The "invisible genie" would give man the leisure to
create at last a culture worthy of his promise. It would validate the nineteenth century's long pursuit of progress. It
would solve the American problem of scarce labor, cleanse
the sooty air of cities such as Pittsburgh and Chicago, and end
the sickening boredom of unmechanized housework. By 1929
Lee DeForest could predict the control of weather and the
instantaneous transmission of moving pictures over long
distances. By the early 1930s 70 percent of the nation's homes
had electricity (though only 10 percent of the farms), and
future applications seemed limitless. What had already happened in a mere half-century of development under private
entrepreneurship was breath-taking. "It is improbable that
all the laws enacted since the days of Caesar," said a University of Chicago astronomer in 1931, "have had so great effects
upon the living conditions of the average man as had [*sic*]
the electrical developments which have taken place entirely
within the memory of many men now living."[1]

The Harding administration's first bill to enable a private takeover of the Muscle Shoals project went, because of its fertilizer provisions, to the Senate Committee on Agriculture. This was a fateful development, for there it fell into the hands of George W. Norris of Nebraska, the committee's chairman. For the next twelve years, Norris attended to the Muscle Shoals problem with unique fidelity, steering it through an incredible maze of legislative dead-ends and nursing it through three hostile administrations until a friendly one finally appeared.

He was equal to the task. Sixty years old in 1921, Norris, born of uneducated parents on an Ohio farm, and had grown up working. "There were weeks," he later wrote, "when there was not a cent in our home."[2] His widowed mother ran the farm, read the Bible straight through to her eleven children once a year, spun all the material for their clothing, and tried to inculcate honesty and ambition. With George, the only male in the family after his brother's death from a Confederate bullet, she succeeded beyond her dreams. He earned his way through Baldwin University and through the law course of what became Valparaiso University. In 1885 he moved to Nebraska, where he practiced law, collected overdue bills, and sold insurance. When economic depression hit the state in the nineties, Norris entered politics. A true believer in Republican orthodoxy (his heroes were the Ohio presidents Hayes and Garfield), he fought the tide of Populism. He served three terms as prosecuting attorney, followed by seven years on the district bench. In 1902 he won a seat in Congress.

Norris served five consecutive terms in the House, then five in the Senate. His forty years of legislative achievement have been matched by few other politicians in American history, if any. His major contributions include the victory of the insurgents over "Czar" Joseph G. Cannon, which reformed the rules of the House; the Anti-injunction Act, which out-lawed the yellow-dog labor contract; the Twentieth Amendment to the Constitution, which ended lame-duck Congresses; the unicameral legislature of Nebraska, which simplified the state's lawmaking process; and the victory for government operation in the Muscle Shoals fight, which culminated in the Tennessee Valley Authority Act of 1933.

Norris did not long remain a standpat Republican. His miserable first years in the House taught him "that my party organization I had supported so vigorously was guilty of virtually all the evils that I had charged against the opposition. One by one, I saw my favorite heroes wither."[3] Committed only to principle, he refused to be bound by his party's caucus, and though his independence deprived him of patronage (which he usually did not want anyway) and certain committee assignments (which he did), it also brought him into contact with likeminded Congressmen. The victory over Cannon in 1910, like some of the Republican insurgents' later triumphs — including Muscle Shoals — came from a combination of patience, righteousness, parliamentary opportunism, and *ad hoc* alliance with the Democratic party.

But Norris's defeats far outnumbered his victories. As one of the "little group of willful men," he filibustered against Wilson's proposal to arm merchant ships. He was one of only six senators who voted against the declaration of war in 1917. And he said incessant nays to the policies of the Republican administrations of the 1920s. For his independence and alleged neglect of Nebraska's interests, powerful men in his party regarded Norris as a turncoat. Yet, despite the frequent opposition of the regular party machinery, his constituents returned him to Washington time after time, until he finally lost his seat in 1942. By 1936 he was no longer even nominally a Republican.

He lived his whole life in the austerity and simplicity with which he began it. Wearing plain black suits, secluded in his office or apartment in Washington, he habitually worked extra hours at his job, educating himself to the technicalities of legislation in which he was interested. No facial peculiarity

could have been more deceptive than Norris's heavily droop-
ing eyelids, which gave him a look of perpetual sleepiness.
No senator had ever been more alert in defense of the public
interest.

Consistent and incorruptible, he was neither a deep nor a
shallow thinker. He sometimes believed what he wanted to
believe, was given to devil-hunting and vehement hatreds,
and regularly denounced his and the public's enemies in
extravagant rhetoric. Melancholy most of the time, Norris
still had a streak of optimism, and he felt with passion the
promise of the Electric Age. "I had lived the hard boyhood
of a primitive Ohio farm," he recalled, "and the possibilities
of electricity for lightening the drudgery of farms and urban
homes, while revolutionizing the factories, fascinated me."[4]

His strongest hatreds, therefore, and his most vicious rhetoric, fell upon those whom he regarded as the corrupters of
the dream — the private power monopolists. With some justification Norris believed they were charging outrageous prices
for electricity in cities and refusing altogether to extend their
power lines into low-profit rural areas. "When this electric age
comes," he wrote in 1926, "we will find ourselves in the grip
of privately owned, privately managed monopoly and it will
be extremely difficult to shake off the shackles that will then
be fastened upon all of us."[5]

Norris had studied the electric business diligently, and he
knew its peculiar economics about as well as any senator did.
He knew that utilities are inherently monopolistic, tending
toward very large units of production and distribution. He
hated monopoly of any kind, but he recognized its inevitability
in the power business. To insist on a return to small units here
would be economically regressive, however satisfying it
might be to the soul of the individual. Therefore, Norris's
habitual reference to the industry as the "power trust," though
effective as reformist rhetoric, was profoundly misleading in
its implications for public policy. To most Americans, trusts
in general seemed bad and competition good. But had the

"power trust" been killed and small competitive units restored, the remedy would have been worse than the disease. The history and nature of the industry suggest why.[6]

Development of the business followed several overlapping patterns. One, a direct outgrowth of the electrical manufacturing enterprises pioneered by the Edison, Thomson-Houston, and Westinghouse companies, pursued what at first blush appears to have been a reverse logic. The companies promoted local power distribution systems to provide markets for their equipment. In this pattern the engineers and the entrepreneurs were often the same persons.

Quick riches provided another motive to build power plants, particularly hydroelectric plants. The notion of "free" power from falling water had immense popular appeal, and J. P. Morgan's personal participation in the sensational Niagara development inspired would-be promoters throughout the country. The hydroelectric mania lost more fortunes than it made; it also brought the federal government into the picture. Many an entrepreneur learned to rue the day he had heard of hydro power.

Feelings of civic responsibility also brought local electrical development. Socially minded businessmen and politicians viewed electric lighting and streetcars as priceless improvements to urban living. Scores of municipally-owned plants were erected on the cities' credit. Though a large number failed financially, they did bring the Electric Age to a number of communities ignored in the first cycle of private initiative. Municipal plants had significant side effects as well. They educated the public in the rudimentary economics of the industry, thereby helping to create an important political issue. In some communities, such as Los Angeles and Seattle, they created a strong and expansionist tradition of public ownership, and an example of very low rates which shamed the private companies. In other areas they resulted in financial confusion which had serious effects on utility accounting, especially in the 1920s, when holding companies purchased large numbers of municipal plants at inflated prices.[7]

The growth of the industry was as amazing as the inventions on which it was based. The power business requires colossal amounts of capital — more than three dollars of plant investment to produce from customers yearly revenues of one dollar. This is about six times the ratio for manufacturing enterprises. The result is that utilities have a very high proportion of fixed costs (such as interest payments and taxes), and are expensive to run regardless of payroll or raw material costs and regardless of whether they operate near capacity. An electric utility cannot store its inventory for better market conditions, because it has no inventory. Its product must be generated, transmitted, delivered, and consumed in virtually the same instant. The business earns a comparatively high rate of return on its income, but a low one on its total investment. That is, a large percentage of the customer's dollar goes to service the huge debts of the companies, but each investor gets a lower return than he would in most other fields.

The security of the investment offsets this disadvantage. Sold under monopolistic conditions, electricity is a necessity, and the revenues it produces are almost as certain as the government's income from taxes. Like governments, most electric utilities never expect to amortize their indebtedness fully, and they remain solvent only by perpetual refinancing. When their bond issues fall due they commonly pay them by selling new bonds. Utilities have also made extensive use of preferred stock, particularly during the boom period of the 1920s, when it sometimes accounted for one-fourth of the capital structure. A relatively secure investment, preferred stock usually carried no voting rights. The combination of bonds and preferred stock often left one-fourth or less of the capital structure in common stock, or "equity," which carried voting rights and control of the company. Ownership of a majority or large minority of the common stock enabled entrepreneurs to control a company capitalized at an amount several times their own investment. This "leverage" was the rule in the 1920s, and it offered all kinds of opportunities for profits, manipulation, and speculation. The scale of operations was grandiose. The spectacular expansion and consolidation of the industry from 1917 to 1930 required thirteen and a half billion dollars of new private capital. This felicitous combination of circumstances — the scale of financing, the built-in leverage, and a product which had caught the imagination of a public entering the Electric Age — proved too much for the country's titans of capital to resist. In the 1920s they plunged in, and the device they employed was the holding company.[8]

Early common law had frowned on the ownership by one corporation of the securities of another. So had the public. John D. Rockefeller's South Improvement scheme was a holding company of unhappy memory. But between 1888 and 1893 the state of New Jersey, anxious to replenish its treasury through corporate residence fees, enacted a series of laws to permit the practice, and the movement began in earnest. Early industrial holding companies included Standard Oil of New Jersey (1899), United States Steel (1901), and Eastman Kodak (1901). The practice spread from industrials to utilities and railways, and finally to commercial banks. The first of the great holding companies in the power business was Electric Bond and Share, formed in 1905 as a subsidiary of General Electric.

Holding companies met a definite economic need. Far-flung operating companies, large and small, had serious problems arising from their continual need for new capital to expand and to replace obsolete equipment (a major annoyance to early power companies). A large, centrally managed holding company had ready access to financial markets where the smaller companies had no standing. Holding companies also facilitated the interchange of power among subsidiary companies, and provided technical, construction, and management services that would have been hard for operating companies individually to afford.

By the time the United States entered World War I, entrepreneurs had consolidated a large proportion of the desirable operating properties under unified management. By and large,

the early holding companies were sound, though their promoters had hardly foreseen the tremendous expansion brought
about by the war, during which the demand for power almost
doubled; or the industrial explosion of the twenties, during
which kilowatt-hour output tripled that of 1917. In the early
phase, holding companies probably benefited operating companies and the public almost as much as they benefited their
own stockholders.

But most of the companies organized from about 1922 onward were something else again. Little besides profit motivated their creation. In the process of consolidation, and afterward too, financiers could make limitless money, from huge
fees and deliberately inflated valuations of the newly combined properties; from pyramiding, or piling atop the operating
companies layers of holding companies, all controlled through
ownership of voting stock multiplied into fantastic leverage;
from dictated contracts, in which the parent company charged
excessive fees for its services; from intercorporate borrowings
("upstream loans"), to the enrichment of the holding company
at the expense of its subsidiary; and from manipulation of
securities in the poorly regulated stock market. Not all holding
companies were guilty of all these practices, but most were
guilty of some. Almost any financial scheme could appear
sound, because the revenues from millions of electric bills
would flow in as regularly as taxes. But the social cost included
a high electric rate for consumers, which not only burdened
the ratepayer but tended to impede the natural business growth
that would have followed progressive rate reductions.

Because of the booming economy, the unsound holding
companies prospered along with the sound. "In short," an
economist wrote, "the industry came to be regarded not only
as one in which it was impossible to lose one's money, but
one in which an increase in security values was to be regarded
as the normal and natural course of affairs."[9] Viewed as safe,
conservative investments, utility stocks and bonds became a
staple of trust funds. That the legatees of such funds were

often widows and orphans provided, in the 1930s, endless grist for the propaganda mill, as the companies denounced the New Deal's alleged destruction of these legitimate investments. In the mid-twenties, the high reputation of the industry itself accounted in part for the attractiveness of its securities. The men who built the power business seemed to have done justice to the promise of the Electric Age. As a feat of engineering the triumph of private enterprise was genuine enough, and the industry deserved its high esteem with the public.

Indeed the industry had taken great pains to raise its reputation even higher. Its spokesman, the National Electric Light Association, conducted a massive public relations campaign to educate the American people about the wonders of electricity and the debt the public owed to the men who had developed the business. "The impelling and underlying motive for constant improvement in the electric light and power field is service," said the executive manager of the NELA in 1922, in a widely distributed speech. "Service is the shibboleth of that industry. All its traditions cluster around it and all its energies are bent to make it, within human limitations, perfect."[10]

The NELA's second major theme was the superior performance of private over public agencies. From its inception the industry had been dominated by towering figures, all of them private entrepreneurs. Most of these men were either engineers or lawyers. A few were financiers. Some had actually founded their companies, and many were still at the helm as the 1930s began. All had just reasons for their sincere and deep conviction that theirs had been careers of service to their communities as well as to their companies. Together they symbolized a powerfully rooted and in many ways admirable private tradition.

In the Muscle Shoals area, the dominant figures were Thomas W. Martin of the Alabama Power Company, Preston Arkwright of the Georgia Power Company, and Josephus

Conn Guild of the Tennessee Electric Power Company. In Detroit the giant was Alex Dow; in Connecticut, Samuel Ferguson; in Milwaukee, John Beggs; in Chicago, Samuel Insull, whose career was a perfect mirror of the industry's career, who symbolized the industry.

Born in England in 1859, Insull emigrated to America in 1881 to become Thomas Edison's private secretary. For a dozen years he was Edison's troubleshooter and intimate, selling the Edison system and managing the inventor's manufacturing and central station interests. After the consolidations which led to General Electric, Insull moved to Chicago and started building his own empire. Technically knowledgeable and financially shrewd, he made his life and his company a model success story. By the 1920s he was a millionaire many times over, chairman of the boards of sixty-five different companies, a respected philanthropist and patron of music, the husband of a well-known actress, and a powerful figure behind the scenes in Chicago and Illinois politics. Engineers recognized his companies as the nation's soundest. Insull had been a leader in virtually every significant development in the industry — in marketing, financing, applications of advancing technology, and particularly public relations. "I am a great believer in publicity," he said in 1919.

> I believe it is our duty to the properties we manage, to the stockholders who own them, and to the communities they serve, that we should enlighten those communities on the situation. I believe in doing it not in any gumshoe way, but openly and boldly.[11]

Insull's sagacious, patriarchal mien, with its flowing white mustaches, was well known to the public, to whom he was one of the great industrial folk heroes of the New Era. In November 1929, *Time* honored him with a cover story.

The occasion was not auspicious. Though Insull appeared to be at the zenith of his success, the Great Crash had come just a week earlier, and his disastrous slide had already begun. When it ended the public learned that he had pyramided and overextended himself to an extent scarcely comprehensible

to the men who tried to pick up the pieces of his broken empire. Disgraced, he fled to Greece, taking with him the shat-
tered dreams of hundreds of thousands of investors. Insull
undertook many of his indiscretions in self-defense against
market-raiding investment bankers, whose entry into the holding company field caused so much trouble. But Insull himself
received the blame. As he had been a symbol of the success
of the twenties, he now became symbol of its failure, a symbol second only to Herbert Hoover. In 1932, the year of his
final collapse, writers denounced him in practically every
magazine and newspaper in the country. In the presidential
campaign of that year, Franklin D. Roosevelt spoke harshly
of the "lone wolf, the unethical competitor, the reckless pro-
moter, the Ishmael or Insull whose hand is against every
man's...."[12]

The rise and fall of Insull's reputation paralleled the rise
and fall of the private tradition's reputation for public service.
It soared in the twenties, started to decline in the decade's
last two years, and hit bottom on the eve of the New Deal. The
cycle derived partly from the industry's own indiscretions,
partly from the boom psychology of the twenties, and partly
from the exertions of a rival and increasingly virile public
tradition.

The public tradition had two components, regulation and
government ownership. They developed independently of
each other, but were closely related. Ultimately they would
merge in the Tennessee Valley Authority.

The two shared a single ideological foundation, resting in
an interpretation of the term "public utility." The phrase had
little currency before the twentieth century, but the idea it
represents is an old one, rooted historically in the common
law and based on economic characteristics of certain enterprises—characteristics which, because they create a need for
public regulation, form the basis of legal definition. One characteristic is necessity, the other is monopoly. On both counts
the electric power business qualifies.

Public utilities have legally enforceable rights and duties. Among the rights are permission to use the streets and other public property, the power of eminent domain (with reasonable compensation), the right to charge rates which will yield a reasonable return, and above all, protection from competition, through possession of a franchise, permit, or license. In the ideology of the public tradition, utilities are special instrumentalities of the political state, exercising quasisovereign powers which make them quite different from other businesses.

In return for these unusual powers, public utilities have certain responsibilities, and are subject to regulation by the local, state, or federal government. Through the police power, the government attempts to insure that they supply all reasonable demands with adequate service; charge reasonable, nondiscriminatory rates within each class of customer; finance, expand, or contract their facilities only with the permission of the regulatory agency; and take care that the public not be endangered by their operations.

In practice, announcing these duties has proved easier than enforcing them. In the early days the regulatory process was haphazard and fragmented, typically involving direct negotiations between the companies and legislative committees or city councils, with infinite chances of corruption. The situation was so bad that often the private tradition itself (Insull led here, too) materially assisted in the organization of state commissions. The state system, which is still in operation, dates from 1907, when New York and Wisconsin established the prototypes of the modern public service commission. By the close of the 1920s almost every state had some kind of commission with jurisdiction over utilities. But the creation of commissions, like so much of the regulatory legislation of the early twentieth century, was more a formal declaration that something had to be done than an effective engagement of the problem.

Overall, despite the efforts of a number of conscientious individual commissioners, the state systems failed. As insti-

tutions they were dwarfed by the companies they were supposed to regulate. They had tiny budgets, small and inexpe-
rienced staffs, ambiguously defined powers, and indifferent
public support. They confronted a labyrinth of legal, engineering, and especially accounting problems. Most important
of all, they were regularly undercut by the federal courts. Judicial decisions were often inconsistent and conflicting, a
source of confusion for the commissions and evasion by the
companies, which could afford to employ the country's finest
legal talent in delays and appeals that proceeded endlessly.

The trouble was rooted in an 1898 landmark decision, *Smyth
v. Ames*.[13] The Supreme Court declared that utilities must be
allowed to earn "a fair return on the fair value of the property
being used." Fair return, after awhile, was no great problem,
and has ever since been set at a number between 5 and 10 percent of the "fair value of property being used." But what is
"fair value"? Is it the cost of original construction? Of repro-
ducing identical facilities later, when prices are inflated? Of
producing equivalent services with better equipment? Of the
company's stocks and bonds? Of its "going value" as an institution? Of the "prudent investment" the properties represent?
At different times the Court said it was, in part, all these things.
Choosing one method over another in individual rate cases
could halve or double the valuation ("rate base"), and thus
halve or double rates.

The valuation problem plagued the commissions, and later
plagued the Tennessee Valley Authority. When it attempted
to purchase privately-owned companies, the TVA would offer
a price based on one method of valuation, and the companies
would propose another method resulting in a much higher
price. For the commissions the valuation problem was almost
unbearable, because it went hand in hand with a propensity
of the courts to review the minutest details of the commissions' methods as well as their decisions. And the advent of
holding companies, whose properties ignored state lines and
commission jurisdictions, was a killing blow, for in the 1920s

no effective federal commission existed. To men like Norris, the conclusion was obvious. The state commissions, the senator wrote in 1926, "can no more contest with this gigantic octopus than a fly could interfere with the onward march of an elephant." To Norris the only recourse was public ownership.[14]

Some upholders of the public tradition believed that state legislatures could make regulation work, through clarification of the commissions' authority, increase in their budgets, inclusion of holding companies in their jurisdictions, and recruitment of better commissioners. Such men as Milo R. Maltbie, who revivified the New York commission in 1930; David E. Lilienthal, who did the same in Wisconsin in 1931; and Morris L. Cooke of Pennsylvania, who had conducted for Governor Gifford Pinchot the Giant Power Survey in the mid-twenties—all agreed that regulation still might work. Though he was friendly with all three of these men, Norris disagreed. "In my judgment," he wrote in 1930, "we will never get regulation which will be satisfactory. The best regulation on earth is to have municipalities go into the business themselves and compete with the power trust. We have some wonderful examples in the United States where that has been done." Where Norris differed from the champions of regulation was not in advocating a limited number of publicly owned municipal systems. They all agreed with him here. But what Norris wanted was complete government ownership of the industry. "If, from the nature of things," he wrote in 1926, "a certain commodity must be a monopoly, then it ought to be owned, controlled, and managed by Government authority." If this put the industry into politics, as the private tradition charged, then the change would be minimal. The private companies had already put themselves into politics as deeply as possible, at every branch and level.[15]

Another source of the public ownership movement was the federal government's operation of hydroelectric projects.

Statistically, hydro power for many years has been less important than steam power, accounting since the 1920s for between
one-sixth and one-third of total kilowatt capacity. Politically
it has been much more important.

Three constitutional provisions involved the federal government in water power. The first was its role as a landowner,
particularly in the West. As late as 1916, for example, the
public domain included 92 percent of Arizona, 84 percent of
Idaho, and 53 percent of California. As an owner, the government had the legal right to power from streams adjacent to its
lands, and it often developed such power incidental to the
irrigation projects of the Bureau of Reclamation. The second
basis of federal jurisdiction was the treatymaking power,
which affects the St. Lawrence, Rio Grande, and Rainy Rivers.
The third, and most important basis, was the government's
power to regulate interstate commerce on navigable rivers.
Ultimately, "navigable" came to mean practically all streams
of any significant size; and interstate commerce applied even
to the waters of a river located entirely within one state.[16]

Despite these clear-cut powers, Congress was slow to develop a policy for hydroelectric development, and the continued uncertainty discouraged private entrepreneurship.
Few guidelines of any kind existed before the passage of the
Federal Water Power Act of 1920. This legislation, the compromise product of a decade-long fight, created the Federal
Power Commission, provided for federal control of water-
power sites, permitted private development through fifty-
year licenses, and authorized charges for the privilege,
payable to the federal treasury. In 1930 Congress reconstituted
the FPC into an independent five-member body, after an awk-
ward ten years during which it consisted of the secretaries of
war, interior, and agriculture. Throughout its history, the
commission's effectiveness in protecting the public interest
has depended on the views of its members. Historically its
record has been distinctly poor, with a few periods of exception, notably during the New Deal.

Norris, Pinchot, and other progressives favored public

development for reasons in addition to power. Viewing rivers as the common heritage of the people, they opposed exploitation for the benefit of corporations. Furthermore, single-purpose private developments, such as hydroelectric dams that blocked river traffic increased flood hazards, made poor economic sense. "To develop a river for navigation alone," Pinchot wrote in 1910, "or power alone, or irrigation alone, is often like using a sheep for mutton, or a steer for beef, and throwing away the leather and the wool." Instead, Pinchot and other conservationists envisioned a government-coordinated development of the nation's rivers as systems. This idea, full of implications for public policy, flowered in the first decade of the twentieth century, but did not bear fruit of any size until the coming of the Tennessee Valley Authority.[17]

To the conservationists, electricity was the keystone of unified resource development, because it would furnish the money to pay for it. Power was the one purpose of a multiple-purpose project that made the dream practical. The construction of a dam creates a power potential whether or not the builder so intends, and it would be a waste of resources, an "economic sin," as Norris often said, not to use the power developed. The idea had a logical integrity that appealed to believers in the gospel of efficiency. But its key, electricity, was the one aspect of river development objectionable to the private tradition.

Public and private interests could be harmonized by the simple expedient of selling the power at wholesale to private companies for distribution to consumers. With certain exceptions, the government followed this policy in its reclamation program and partly at Boulder Dam, which was, like Muscle Shoals, a political battleground in the twenties.[18] But this practice enabled corporations to profit from the public development of resources that belonged to the public in the first place, and was therefore unacceptable to the conservationists.

Aside from the socialists, few persons of influence or prominence were prepared to declare, like Norris, for complete government ownership of the power industry. But many were allied with Norris on Muscle Shoals, because it represented the phase of the power question best adaptable to several designs — to regulation by example (the "yardstick" idea); to municipal ownership (power from Wilson Dam to be distributed by municipalities near the dam); and to the gospel of conservation and unified river development. The Muscle Shoals issue united practically all defenders of the public tradition — the great engineers of the municipal systems, such as E. F. Scattergood of Los Angeles, who fought the power companies for decades, and J. D. Ross of Seattle, who in the thirties would serve on the Securities and Exchange Commission and the Bonneville Power Administration; progressive Republicans such as Fiorello La Guardia of New York and the anti-Insull reformers Harold Ickes and Donald Richberg of Chicago; Socialist party members such as Harry Laidler and Norman Thomas; public power senators such as Charles McNary of Oregon, Clarence Dill of Washington, and Thomas Walsh of Montana; and propagandists such as Judson King of the National Popular Government League and Carl Thompson of the Public Ownership League.

But the private tradition also spoke with one voice on Muscle Shoals. The issue was squarely joined. Each group was too weak to win but too strong to lose, and so stalemate persisted for a dozen years.

When Norris began his fight in the early twenties, he strove for stalemate. For the time being, the public power forces were far too weak to hope for quick victory. "If for no other reason than the conservative tendencies of those years," Norris later wrote, he had to overcome "a nearly insurmountable barrier." Since almost everyone accepted the dogma that private enterprise had built America, "Governmental operation and ownership was looked upon with great suspicion, distaste, and open resentment."[19]

In March 1921, the new Harding administration announced

that if private industry would guarantee a return commensurate with the investment at Muscle Shoals, then the government would complete the dam and lease the whole project. Despite stirrings of interest from the Alabama Power Company, which had owned the damsite before the war, the first important bid came from outside the power industry—from Henry Ford, the number one industrial folk hero of the period.[20]

With a great flourish, Ford offered to take over the project, operate it for the benefit of fertilizer-seeking farmers, and develop Muscle Shoals into one of the industrial centers of the nation. But a close reading of Ford's offer disclosed a certain vagueness of detail. The proposal legally bound him to do practically nothing. Besides, it contemplated gross violations of the recently passed Federal Water Power Act, and payment to the government of a price accurately described by Norris as a "mere bagatelle."

But the Ford name was magic in the twenties, and the proposal won support from the American Federation of Labor, the *New York Times*, the American Farm Bureau Federation, and most Democrats in Congress and out, particularly those from the South. Ford himself, whose explicit "desire for great public service" and "industrial philanthropy" at Muscle Shoals may have had some connection with the contemporaneous Ford for President movement, took the occasion to indulge his remarkable zaniness. He promised vaguely to build a city employing a million men, and institute a new Muscle Shoals currency based on the "energy dollar," which would vitiate the influence of Wall Street and international Jewry. This in turn would end wars by eliminating dependence on their cause, which was gold. Accompanied by the aged and approving Thomas Edison, Ford made a highly publicized tour of the area which sent local excitement into a frenzy. His interest in Muscle Shoals touched off a real estate boom, and miles of new streets materialized in expectation of a new Detroit. Rumors spread that Ford would employ the entire work force of Alabama, that he would halve the price of commercial fertilizer and give away a free ton with each new Model T, and that he would singlehandedly solve the nation's agriculture problem.

In the end Henry Ford's dream of a southern empire died in the Senate, a victim not of "Wall Street," as Ford said, but of a coalition of his diverse enemies—Norris and his cohorts; the power companies, whose slumbering interest had awakened with a start; and the fertilizer "trust," which opposed production of their commodity at Muscle Shoals by anyone.

The defeat of Ford consumed three years and left advocates of public and private power as the major contestants. Norris's work had just begun. He now had to battle a bill introduced by Senator Underwood of Alabama closely modeled on the Ford plan; another measure recommended by the Coolidge-appointed Muscle Shoals Inquiry Commission, which differed little from the Underwood bill; still another bill recommended by the Joint Committee on Muscle Shoals to lease the dam to power companies; and finally a bill to lease the properties to the American Cyanamid Company. Of these, the Cyanamid bill was the most important. It proposed to give the company broad powers not just at Muscle Shoals but along the entire length of the river. As the early reports of an exhaustive U.S. Army Corps of Engineers study showed, the Tennessee had power possibilities far beyond Muscle Shoals. Begun in the twenties, the Corps' survey laid much of the technical groundwork for the projects of the Tennessee Valley Authority, saving that agency much time and money.

The successive elimination of these schemes enhanced the prospects for Norris's plan, and he lost no time in getting his bills onto the floor of Congress. In session after session, beginning in 1922, his proposals, relentlessly introduced, began to pick up votes. By 1928 his chances began for the first time to look good. They were helped immeasurably by a combination of peculiar circumstances, two of them old and one new. First, Congress had to do something with the dam and nitrate plants. They were enormously expensive, cost money to maintain, and returned next to nothing. Second, the farm bloc insisted that somebody, anybody, operate the nitrate plants for fertilizer. Third, the long decline of the power industry's reputation had begun and would soon reach the point of nationwide revulsion. It was stimulated most effectively by the first reports of an investigation by the Federal Trade Commission which had, in part, grown out of the Muscle Shoals fight itself. In 1930, the House Interstate Commerce Committee began its own investigation of holding companies, heaping fuel on an already roaring fire.

The Federal Trade Commission's study was the most intensive inquiry into the affairs of a particular industry in American history. Ultimately it consumed seven years' time. Its reports appeared in regular and seemingly interminable monthly installments to the Senate and finally in eighty-odd published volumes of analysis and exhibits. It inspired countless news stories, editorials, and magazine articles. It furnished the principal source for at least six contemporary books, with such titles as *Confessions of the Power Trust, High Power Propaganda,* and *The Public Pays.*[21] The investigation almost completely demolished the private tradition's reputation for public service. To Norris, it was a godsend.

The investigation disclosed that individually and through the National Electric Light Association, the power companies had for years engaged in every conceivable medium of publicity and propaganda: books, pamphlets, textbooks, circulars, news bulletins, canned editorials, law reporting; subsidy of a few teachers, newspapermen, and school officials; widespread customer "ownership" campaigns to sell nonvoting stock; appearances of utility spokesmen on radio shows, club, school, church, and college programs; everything, as the NELA's publicity director said, except skywriting. The reason for the colossal expenditure of energy and money was obvious. Without it, as one utility publicist noted in 1925, "We'd all be in a hell of a shape. . . . Without this, I venture to say that State, municipal, and Government ownership would have been 100 percent ahead of what it is today."[22]

Few of the utilities' critics would deny them the freedom to tell what was, after all, a remarkable success story. But much of the publicity concerned politics as well as kilowatts—the horrors of government ownership, which the NELA characterized as Bolshevistic, socialistic, inefficient, and generally odious; and the contrasting accomplishments of private enterprise, which gave free rein to individual initiative under the alert eyes of state regulatory commissions. The NELA habitually labored to get its message across in disguise, through canned editorials or ghost-written articles over the signatures of prominent citizens. As a final insult the public paid for its own indoctrination. Utility accountants normally charged off propaganda costs as operating expenses, in the same manner as salaries or fuel.

The association movement of the twenties, of which the NELA was a part, was vigorously promoted by Herbert Hoover, first as secretary of commerce, then as president. As a whole, the movement produced many benefits. Hundreds of socially minded businessmen participated. Franklin D. Roosevelt, for example, worked with Hoover to set up the American Construction Council, and served as its president for seven years. But Hoover himself was the spirit behind the movement.

He spoke at the NELA's conventions in 1922, 1924, and 1925, and brought pleasant messages. "Being one who believes that the progress of our nation can come," he said at the convention in 1924,

> only by preserving on one hand that vital initiative and enterprise of our people and on the other an equality of opportunity to all, I necessarily do not favor the strangulation of both by the hand of bureaucracy and politics. No bureaucracy with a board

of directors of 580 Congressmen and Senators would have made the electrical discoveries of the last 50 years or pioneered their application.

And in 1925: "It is my belief that the [state] public service commissions with very little just criticism are proving themselves fully adequate to control the situation."[23]

With this kind of support from government spokesmen, the NELA confidently moved forward in its campaign to propagate self-serving ideas. In scope the campaign was huge. None approaching it, judged the FTC, "has ever been conducted except possibly by governments in war time." (The comparison was apt. In Illinois, Insull adapted the war propaganda machinery, which he himself had set up, to power companies' use right after the Armistice.) Except for its magnitude, the NELA's campaign resembled those of dozens of other trade associations. But the NELA represented a public utility, with all the powers and responsibilities the term implies. When it began to sell a philosophy as well as a service, it overreached itself.[24]

By 1933 the FTC investigators and their numerous literary progeny had brought the NELA into such disrepute that the industry gave up altogether and dissolved the association, replacing it with a successor attractively styled the "Edison Electric Institute." The founders of the EEI declared that the new association would "divest itself of all semblance of propaganda activities" and "assume an attitude of frankness and ready cooperation in its dealings with the public." If any further evidence of the sins of the NELA was needed, this announcement provided it. Soon the unobjectionable "Reddy Kilowatt" appeared and for a time the Edison Electric Institute kept its promise of good, or at least apolitical, behavior.[25]

Muscle Shoals had been a particular target of propaganda, and the NELA's disgrace helped Norris's cause no end. On December 15, 1927, he introduced his bill again. It ran into trouble in the Senate with a filibuster and in the House with a substitute measure, but after much agitation and delay it passed both houses near the end of the session in 1928. Most of the votes came from southern Democrats and western Republicans. "The problem of Muscle Shoals," President Coolidge had said in 1925, to the disgust of southerners and conservationists, "seems to me to have assumed a place all out of proportion with its real importance. It probably does not represent in market value much more than a first-class battleship. . . . " When the bill reached him for signature in 1928 he gave it a pocket veto. Norris lost again.[26]

The election of Herbert Hoover brought no change of executive policy. In his first message to Congress on the subject, Hoover recommended leasing Muscle Shoals to private entrepreneurs, a course of action Congress had already rejected several times. His patience beginning to wear thin, Norris again introduced his bill. Again it passed near the end of a session, and Hoover had the option of a pocket veto. Unlike Coolidge, he declined to evade the issue. Hoover favored most conservation projects, but Muscle Shoals meant government in business as well. His veto message, very powerfully worded, was as clear an expression of the philosophy of the private tradition as had ever appeared:

> I am firmly opposed to the Government entering into any business the major purpose of which is competition with our citizens. . . . for the Federal Government deliberately to go out to build up and expand such. . . . a power and manufacturing business is to break down the initiative and enterprise of the American people; it is the destruction of equality of opportunity amongst our people, it is the negation of the ideals upon which our civilization has been based. . . . The power problem is not to be solved by the Federal Government going into the power business. . . . I hesitate to contemplate the future of our institutions, of our Government, and of our country if the preoccupation of its officials is to be no longer the promotion of justice and equal opportunity but is to be devoted to barter in the markets. That is not liberalism, it is degeneration.[27]

Hoover proposed a joint Alabama-Tennessee commission, which the states duly appointed. The commission made its study and its recommendations, but the process was a charade. Hoover's veto came in 1931. By then events had outrun ideology, and the economic depression had begun to work its profound political effects. One of these would be a resolution, at long last, of the Muscle Shoals problem. But for the time being, the legislature and the executive still could not agree, and the private and public traditions remained at stalemate. Norris bided his time.

2

THE PRESIDENT AND THE DIRECTORS

NOWHERE IN THE COUNTRY did the public and private traditions confront each other as directly as in New York state. Here was the home of Edison's original central station, of the prototype regulatory commission, of General Electric, of the capital market, of most holding companies, of one of the greatest hydroelectric potentials east of the Mississippi. And facing New York, just across Niagara Falls, stood the continent's single magnificent example of regional public power, the Ontario Hydroelectric Commission. Ontario Hydro's almost unbelievably low residential rates furnished constant embarrassment to the utility interests of New York, and good factual ammunition to public power propagandists across the nation. It was natural, therefore, that no governor (with Pinchot of Pennsylvania a possible exception), spent so much of his time on the power question as did Franklin D. Roosevelt of New York.[1]

His interest in the problem long antedated his governorship. At Harvard he had studied under the redoubtable William Z. Ripley, much of whose course in the economics of transportation applied to public utilities in general. At Columbia Law School he had earned one of his better grades, a B, in Jackson Reynolds's course in public utility law.[2] The power question included several of the subjects most interesting to Roosevelt: conservation, government-in-business, corporate finance, public regulation, and rural life.

26

Infused with the potent image of the Electric Age, the power issue had some appeal to every voter who paid an electric bill, and much more to those who did not—to housewives without appliances and to farmers without prospect of getting their homes and barns wired as long as the motive for electrification was not service but profit. During his four years at Albany, 1929–1933, few issues provided Roosevelt with such political capital. The utilities were invaluable political enemies, and in New York they were unusually visible. The headquarters of most holding companies was Wall Street. The state Republican chairman was a power magnate. The chairman of the public service commission was a man whose self-defined role was mediator between the public and the companies rather than the public's advocate, and who finally ended his feud with Roosevelt by resigning.

Roosevelt exploited his opportunities to the fullest. Though his policy sometimes varied, his rhetoric never did. At every opportunity he hammered relentlessly at the utilities and their holding companies. He sent Louis Howe around the state and into Ontario collecting data on electric bills and gleefully quoted the results of Howe's research: that a family using a certain amount of electricity would have to pay $17.50 per month in Manhattan, $19.50 in Albany, $7.80 in Buffalo, $6.93 in Dunkirk, which had a municipal plant, and less than $3.00 anywhere in Ontario, with its regional public power system.[3] The FTC investigation and the Muscle Shoals fight made it the best time ever to be against the excesses of the private tradition. The utility men were outstanding symbols of an era growing in disrepute, of the financial "double-shuffling, honey-fugling, hornswoggling, and skulduggery," as FDR's old teacher William Z. Ripley called it, of the 1920s.[4] After the crash, none of it seemed very funny.

Roosevelt's governorship amounted to a postgraduate education in the public tradition. At Albany he dealt directly and almost constantly with its two constituent parts—with public ownership, represented by the fight over St. Lawrence hydropower; and with regulation, embodied in his running battle with the utility commission. In addition, his experience with a rudimentary form of regional planning for New York convinced him that much more than electricity was involved in the national issue of Muscle Shoals. Though he never developed a genuinely coherent philosophy of regional planning, his experience produced some important new provisions in what would be the last of the Norris Muscle Shoals bills.

The fight over St. Lawrence power had dragged on for a quarter of a century before FDR became governor, emerging into a major issue during the administration of Al Smith. As at Muscle Shoals, the public and private traditions (and the executive and legislature) were stalemated. The problem was further complicated by the superior jurisdiction of the federal government over the river, which forms an international boundary. Whatever the state might want to do, the Harding and Coolidge administrations would not permit a public power program on the St. Lawrence.

Roosevelt achieved a bit more than had Smith, but the conditions that frustrated his predecessor frustrated him as well. He probably knew that the legislature and the Hoover administration would allow him to get nowhere, especially as the 1932 election approached and he emerged as Hoover's likely opponent. Roosevelt could do little more than keep the issue alive, educate the public about it, and reap the political dividends. Sometimes his statements of policy temporized. Although he consistently asserted the people's ownership of water power (almost everyone since Theodore Roosevelt had gone that far), he advocated state operation only as an extreme resort. Never did he propose a broad program of public ownership, as Norris had done in Congress, and he endorsed Norris's Muscle Shoals plan only tentatively.

Yet he did achieve a major moral victory, and minor substantive victories. He tamed the power magnates by skillful manipulation of public opinion, and he outmaneuvered the legislature in getting a St. Lawrence Commission whose report followed his policies. As the commission recommended, he then appointed a New York Power Authority, a body originally proposed by Al Smith, charged with solving the St. Lawrence problem. The Power Authority was an agency of extraordinary competence, but for the time being the State Department and the New York legislature tied its hands. Ultimately the St. Lawrence controversy consumed another quarter-century, into Roosevelt's presidency and beyond.

On the question of regulation and ratemaking, Roosevelt was more successful. A student of public utility law, he knew that the criterion "fair rate of return on fair value" was a totally inadequate and ambiguous basis for effective regulation. He therefore proposed that the state commission be investigated and its powers strengthened, and that the reproduction-cost theory of valuation be immediately replaced by the prudent-investment standard enunciated by Justice Louis D. Brandeis. On the question of the power someday to be generated by the waters of the St. Lawrence, Roosevelt proposed that, in view of the ineffectiveness of the Public Service Commission, it be bypassed altogether. He suggested instead a fixing of rates by contract between the state, which would generate the power, and the private companies, which would distribute it at retail. This principle, though moot in New York because the St. Lawrence was not developed, was adopted in 1933 by the Tennessee Valley Authority. The TVA stipulated by contract the retail rates at which its power would be sold by municipalities and cooperative distributors. It was the keystone of the TVA's power policy, and the point at which the two branches of the public tradition, regulation and government ownership, merged in a single instrument. Roosevelt opposed broad government ownership of the utility industry, but enthusiastically endorsed the public tradition's conception of what "public utility" meant. "The whole question, in my mind," he wrote in 1929, "is as to whether a public utility has the right to make any old profit that it can or not, in other words, as to whether there is any real distinction between a public utility company and a purely private business."[5] Extremely critical of holding companies, Roosevelt wanted a reinvigoration of the regulatory process, if necessary involving limited government ownership for purposes of a "yardstick."

The word "yardstick" arose frequently in Congress and the press in connection with the Muscle Shoals fight. Like "power trust" and "fair value," it had great emotive force, enormous popularity, and an ambiguous meaning. It expressed the most facile and appealing idea associated with the impending TVA power program, but as a slogan produced no end of confusion, recrimination, and distortion, on both sides.

Roosevelt privately claimed to have invented the term.[6] His first experience with the idea came in 1914, when, as Assistant Secretary of the Navy, he debated with his chief, Josephus Daniels, the propriety of erecting a government steel plant to ascertain the cost of producing armor-plate, on which three contractors had submitted identical bids. Foregoing an appeal to the antitrust laws, the infuriated Daniels wanted the government to build a plant large enough to supply the Navy's entire needs. Roosevelt proposed instead a smaller, demonstration plant so that, as the official report stated, the Department could discover "by actual experience the prices the Navy should pay for such products when secured from private contractors." The yardstick idea fascinated Roosevelt, and he later advocated it not only for the power industry but for barge traffic, "as an economic adjunct, to keep a check on what transportation should cost."[7]

At first glance, a government yardstick seemed especially appropriate for the power problem, since a major difficulty in ratemaking was determining cost of production. Actually the idea was particularly invalid for the power business, because a government plant would automatically avoid much of the huge fixed interest costs paid by private operators. And when applied to a multiple purpose enterprise such as the TVA, the notion contained a deep and irreconcilable paradox. But none of this was apparent at first, and the yardstick con-

tinued to be a popular and important justification for the
Muscle Shoals project and for public power in general.

As with Daniels and armor-plate, so with Norris and public
ownership. Roosevelt wanted a yardstick, not a complete
government takeover. Nor did his anti-utility rhetoric approach
Norris's in vehemence. Yet by 1932 FDR too had emerged as
a leading critic of the power trust. And of the men who had a
real chance for the presidency, he was by far the most knowledgeable on the utility question. "In power, 'he knows his
stuff' and quickly gets the fine distinctions," wrote Morris L.
Cooke. "Here was a subject," recalled Raymond Moley, "to
which Roosevelt had given more painstaking study than he
had to any other single one." And Judson King of the National
Popular Government League wrote Norris that "Outside
yourself I have never met an official in public life that has a
firmer grip upon the technical requirements of the electrical
fight that are necessary to produce cheap rates and make it a
success."[8]

Before he clarified his position during the 1932 campaign,
the truest index of Roosevelt's thinking was neither his policies nor his rhetoric, but the men he consulted and appointed.
To the New York Power Authority he named Frank P. Walsh,
Morris L. Cooke, James C. Bonbright, and Leland Olds, all
of them bitter opponents of the utility magnates. Basil Manly,
an economist and public power advocate who had directed
the People's Legislative Service in the twenties, became the
Power Authority's Washington representative. FDR named
Milo R. Maltbie as the new chairman of the New York Public
Service Commission. A member of the original 1907 commission, Maltbie was one of the best known champions of the
public tradition in the country. And informally, Roosevelt
consulted with Professor Felix Frankfurter of the Harvard
Law School, whom he had known since the early days of the
first Wilson administration.[9]

Every one of these men would become important in the
New Deal's utility fight. Walsh and Bonbright would continue

for years on the Power Authority, and Maltbie on the Public
Service Commission. Bonbright was even then preparing, in
collaboration with another Columbia economist, an important
and critical book on holding companies; he would become a
consultant for TVA on electric rates. Cooke would be the
first head of the Rural Electrification Administration. Olds
and Manly would go to the Federal Power Commission. Frankfurter would exert powerful influence directly and through
his many proteges.

Hoover and Roosevelt, the candidates in 1932, were as
far apart on the power question as they were on any issue.
Hoover's resounding veto of the Muscle Shoals bill made
him unattractive to public power enthusiasts, and Roosevelt's
performance in New York was appealing. Yet, as the campaign
progressed, FDR seemed willing to let his record speak for
him. Since his record was not free of ambiguity, and since he
had been, as Norris complained, "practically silent on that
subject" since his nomination, he left himself open to attack.
The Nation criticized him, as did Norman Thomas, the Socialist candidate who had long derided his halfway measures in
New York. To Roosevelt's defense came Judson King of the
National Popular Government League, the nonpartisan progressive lobby founded in 1913 and consisting mainly of King
and his wife. The thorough analysis in a twenty-four-page
pamphlet issued by King found FDR right and Hoover wrong
on each of ten specific issues, such as control of holding companies, valuation methods, and recognition of the right of
public operation. King especially praised Roosevelt's appointments to the Power Authority, which "is in personnel one
of the most outstanding commissions of recent years and its
membership must weigh heavily as determining Roosevelt's
sincerity and courage in the power fight."[10]

On September 21, 1932, FDR finally gave the "concrete il-
lustration" of his position that Norris had wanted. In a campaign speech at public-power conscious Portland, Oregon, he
delivered the most thorough exposition of his attitudes he had

ever given or would ever give. Throughout the thirties, the makers of New Deal power policy recurred again and again to this address, and it became famous as "the Portland speech." It was a document of the first importance.

"I do not hold," said the candidate, conscious of a need to head off charges of socialism, "with those who advocate Government ownership or Government operation of all utilities. I state to you categorically that as a broad general rule the development of utilities should remain, with certain exceptions, a function for private initiative and private capital." The exceptions were local systems owned by municipalities and hydro sites owned by the government. If a community became dissatisfied with the service rendered by the private company, it had "the undeniable basic right" to set up its own service, after a fair referendum. As for state or federal hydro development, the government could not only generate the power but had the right "to go further and to transmit and distribute where reasonable and good service is refused by private capital. . . ." This gives to the people an "essential 'birch rod' in the cupboard." As Roosevelt well knew, the power to transmit electricity was crucial, for if the public developer lacked the authority to build transmission lines, he lacked the means for getting his product to market. He depended on the initiative of others to build the lines to him. In most cases this meant whatever private company operated in the area.[11]

Roosevelt demanded thorough federal regulation of holding companies, then turned to the yardstick. "Here you have the clear picture of four great Government power developments in the United States—the St. Lawrence River in the Northeast, Muscle Shoals in the Southeast, the Boulder Dam project in the Southwest, and finally, but by no means the least of them, the Columbia River in the Northwest. Each one of these, in each of the four quarters of the United States, will be forever a national yardstick to prevent extortion against the public and to encourage the wider use of that servant of the people – electric power." Roosevelt outlined several ways to make regulation more effective, disparaged the "Insull monstrosity," and observed that the power question intimately affected the everyday lives of citizens. The progress of the Electric Age had wrought a great change. "Cold figures do not measure the human importance of the electric power in our present social order. Electricity is no longer a luxury. It is a definite necessity." "Judge me," he said in closing, "by the enemies I have made. Judge me by the selfish purposes of these utility leaders who have talked of radicalism while they were selling watered stock to the people and using our schools to deceive the coming generation."[12]

Norris was elated. Roosevelt's specific mention of Muscle Shoals as a yardstick area and his endorsement of public transmission lines meant that if the senator could shepherd his bill through Congress just once more, and if Roosevelt won the election, then the dozen years of fighting would end in total victory. In 1932, as the depression became deeper and deeper, both conditions appeared very good bets indeed. The policies set forth in the Portland speech, Norris exulted, would "put the power trust out of business." They would also put the government into business. At Madison Square Garden, a haggard Herbert Hoover said, "In that bill was the flat issue of the federal government permanently in competitive busi-ness. I vetoed it because of that principle and not because it especially applied to electric power." But Hoover's views no longer mattered very much. The election returns only confirmed what he and most of his party expected.[13]

Before the inauguration Roosevelt invited Norris to tour the Tennessee Valley with him, and the senator happily ac-cepted. At the end of the long trip to Muscle Shoals, as they stood looking at Wilson Dam (FDR for the first time and Norris for the first time in a decade), the president-elect said, "This ought to be a happy day for you, George." Norris, now past seventy, denied newspapermen's reports that there were tears in his eyes. "Is he really with you?" reporters asked the old man after the return to Washington. "He is more than with me, because he plans to go even farther than I did."[14]

A speech at Montgomery during the trip foreshadowed just how much farther Roosevelt did plan to go: "Muscle Shoals gives us the opportunity to accomplish a great purpose for the people of many States and, indeed, for the whole Union. Because there we have an opportunity of setting an example of planning, not just for ourselves but for the generations to come, tying in industry and agriculture and forestry and flood prevention, tying them all into a unified whole over a distance of a thousand miles so that we can afford better opportunities and better places for living for millions of yet unborn in the days to come." The president's message to Congress a month after the inauguration continued this theme. Muscle Shoals was but one part of the potential usefulness of the river. "Such use, if envisioned in its entirety, transcends mere power development; it enters the wide fields of flood control, soil erosion, afforestation, elimination from agricultural use of marginal lands, and distribution and diversification of industry." Wilson Dam, a relic of the war, "leads logically to national planning for a complete river watershed involving many States and the future lives and welfare of millions. It touches and gives life to all forms of human concerns."[15]

This approach to Muscle Shoals is directly traceable not only to the progressive conservationists but to FDR's land-use planning in New York state. It gave the Norris measure much broader scope. In the TVA bill, introduced the day after Roosevelt sent up his message, appeared two short new sections that seemed to give the president authority to do a great many things, all under the ambiguous head "planning." These provisions were the work of Arthur E. Morgan, a well-known hydraulic engineer from Ohio, whom Roosevelt had already selected to head the new Tennessee Valley Authority.[16]

But the fight over the bill in Congress had nothing to do with the planning sections. It centered, as it had in the past, on the notion of government in the power business. The men already in the power business in the Tennessee Valley protested that there was too much power in the area, and that more hydroelectric construction would be a great social waste. "May I say," Preston Arkwright of Georgia Power told the House committee, "that I do not think we need additional lines, and no power is needed to serve that territory generally." The market for the government's electricity, said James Longley of Tennessee Electric Power, "of necessity comes from the communities that are already served by the privately owned companies." "When the markets go, the companies are gone," said E. A. Yates, vice-president of the Commonwealth and Southern Corporation, the holding company which owned the Georgia, Alabama, Tennessee, and Mississippi companies then serving the area. (Yates would become famous in the 1950s as one-half of Dixon-Yates.) And the president of the Commonwealth and Southern, an affable, impressive man named Wendell L. Willkie, laid the issue squarely on the line. The stocks and bonds of his companies would collapse under government competition. "I do not want to be in the position of an alarmist," said Willkie, "and I do not want to overstate any situation, but I can say to you, as my deliberate judgment, that if this bill passes, this $400,000,000 worth of securities will be eventually destroyed." Partly as a result of this hostile testimony, there was a short, stiff fight in the House over the authorization for transmission lines. But the critical powers stayed in the bill, chiefly owing to the efforts of Norris and the direct intervention of Roosevelt. On May 18, 1933, the president signed the Tennessee Valley Authority Act. After twelve years of unremitting battle, Senator Norris had finally driven his enemies from the field. It was a complete victory.[17]

The battle in Congress was over, but the battle in the Valley had hardly begun. Those who welcomed TVA mainly as an instrument to chastise the power trust would sometimes find their single-minded interest conflicting not only with the private tradition but also with the other missions entrusted to the TVA.

Arthur E. Morgan, Roosevelt's choice as chairman of the new agency, was a man of many talents who consistently held to the vision of the Authority as a broad, multipurpose enterprise. This view made him unpopular with several more determined opponents of the power magnates, but it accorded well with the task at hand in 1933, and with Roosevelt's own conception of the TVA. On the power question, Morgan was a moderate, like Roosevelt. Fifty-five years old in 1933, he was the president of Antioch College, and a nationally known hydraulic engineer.[18]

After a difficult and somewhat sickly and introspective childhood in St. Cloud, Minnesota, Morgan had started his career as an assistant to his father, who was a surveyor. He decided to become a water-control engineer because he lacked the formal education necessary in older fields of engineering. With great diligence he quickly became an expert, and by 1910 had helped frame new drainage codes for several states and had set up his own firm, the Morgan Engineering Company of Memphis, Tennessee. For the next twenty years he supervised about seventy projects scattered over every section of the country.

Beginning in 1913, the Morgan firm tackled its greatest assignment: the planning and construction of a huge flood control project for the Miami River Valley in Ohio, in the aftermath of a disastrous flood that nearly ruined Dayton and several smaller cities as well. For the Ohio legislature Morgan drafted a unique bill which became the Miami Conservancy Act, organizing the area into a cooperative district. The project was financially self-liquidating, and the district's governing board exercised powers of eminent domain. Morgan's remarkable resourcefulness and bold use of some untried flood control methods earned him a national reputation and a long list of eager clients.

His career as an educator, equally successful, began when Morgan became a trustee of Antioch College, then a tiny and almost bankrupt school in Yellow Springs, Ohio. He immediately set out to bring the institution's performance into line with the promise envisioned by its founder, Horace Mann, who in 1853 had established what he hoped would become a western Harvard.

Morgan quickly took the helm himself, assuming the presidency of Antioch in 1920. With the financial support of Charles Kettering and other prominent businessmen, he attempted to make the college an exemplar of a new kind of higher education in America. Infused with a cooperative and communitarian spirit, he instituted the work-study program for which the school became famous, and set up campus industries in which students could apply their academic lessons. He wanted a community at Antioch as well as a school. All colleges, Morgan believed, should take note of changing twentieth-century conditions, analyze their educational purpose, then "design, as engineers designed the first automobile, such an assemblage of methods and resources as will best fulfill that purpose."[19]

James M. Cox, Roosevelt's old running mate from 1920, suggested Morgan for the TVA chairmanship. Governor of Ohio during the Miami Valley project, Cox well remembered Morgan's great achievement. Roosevelt already knew of the innovations at Antioch. Eleanor Roosevelt had offered to serve on a New York fund-raising committee for the college, and during their years in Albany the Roosevelts had received Morgan's semimonthly publication *Antioch Notes*, a pamphlet in which he delivered homiletic and sometimes self-evident messages of social uplift and philosophical speculation.

As educator and as engineer, Morgan was one of a kind. Utopian, ascetic, almost mystical, he inspired powerful loyalty in many of his students and associates, mild contempt and dubiety in others. He had much in common with the

Utopian Socialists of the nineteenth century, and some with
the Puritan divines of the seventeenth, but he was neither a
socialist nor a Christian. As a thinker he was creative and
moralistic, deeply convinced of his own righteousness and
of its great power. Viewing both government and education
as empirical engineering problems, he sometimes chafed at
human frailty. But the extraordinary range of his genius was
a fitting match for the range of Roosevelt's ambitions for the
Tennessee Valley Authority. Morgan looked forward to the
fulfillment of the Authority's multiple purposes with soaring
enthusiasm. The TVA, he said in 1933, "is the kind of thing I
have been wanting to do all my life."[20]

The TVA Act provided for a governing board of three directors, with staggered nine-year appointments, salaries of
$10,000, exceedingly broad discretionary powers, and unde-
fined distinction between the chairman and his two associates.
The directors must believe in the "feasibility and wisdom"
of the Act, and could have no financial interest in a fertilizer,
power, or other business connected with TVA's missions.
They were to administer a government corporation, free of
civil service laws and unconnected with regular federal departments. Their stewardship to Congress was operative only
in the matter of appropriations. Their direct superior was the
president.[21]

When he signed the Act in May 1933, Roosevelt had selected only Morgan, who had already been at work for a month,
appointing on his own several key staff members and, at
Roosevelt's request, looking for other board members. The
president stipulated that one should be familiar with electric
power and the other with agriculture, preferably southern
agriculture. Morgan conducted a meticulous search, traveling
all over the country for interviews. After six weeks' intensive
looking, he was ready with recommendations. The southern
agriculturist he found in Harcourt A. Morgan, the sixty-five-
year-old president of the University of Tennessee, who had

the warm endorsement of officials in the Department of Agriculture, the Russell Sage Foundation, and several land grant colleges. Like Arthur Morgan, to whom he was unrelated. Harcourt Morgan possessed an honorary doctoral degree and was a college president. The confusion was resolved in the early TVA by differentiating the two as "Dr. A. E. and Dr. H. A."

Born and educated in Canada, Harcourt Morgan had moved to Louisiana, where he taught entomology at the state university and helped run the new agricultural experiment station. He was an expert on crop pests, and conducted several noteworthy battles against boll weevils, army worms, cattle ticks, and grasshoppers. In 1905 he went to Knoxville as head of the University of Tennessee's agricultural experiment station. Morgan got along unusually well with southern farmers. He lectured at Farmers' Institutes throughout the state, cajoled his students into using progressive methods, and traveled on horseback recruiting young men for the university's new agricultural college. As he entered middle age, his career began a rapid rise. In 1913 he became dean of the college of agriculture, served as Tennessee's Food Administrator during the war, became president of the university in 1919, and was elected in 1927 president of the Association of Land Grant Colleges and Universities.

Morgan's only true love was agriculture, and slowly he evolved a philosophy of natural resources he called "The Common Mooring." He was often inarticulate, and though his definition of the Common Mooring seemed abstruse even to his closest associates, its essence was simple enough: man is only a part of nature, no more and no less important than other parts. When one part receives undue emphasis, nature's unity disappears and disaster results. The imbalance of southern agriculture had produced such a disaster, and set off an economic chain reaction that injured industry and commerce as well as agriculture. For Morgan, TVA's broad program of unified resource development, to which he himself contributed basic doctrine, was a priceless opportunity to restore balance, through what he called "the integration of natural and human resources."[22]

For the project to succeed, Morgan believed that the "human resources" of the Tennessee Valley must believe TVA to be a good thing. He felt with some passion that genuine progress depended on patient indoctrination, and he conceived of TVA as the agent of an "educational process" which would succeed only if it commandeered "the diversified talent of the Valley in all its activities." Because of his conviction that quick, radical agricultural readjustment was impossible, Harcourt Morgan's reformism, unlike Chairman Arthur Morgan's, was fundamentally conservative.[23]

As liaison between the Valley and the TVA, there could have been few better selections than H. A. Morgan, whose lanky frame, easy conversation, and leathery face typified the farmers he represented. Enormously popular and politically shrewd, he had wheedled unusual sums for the university from a miserly state legislature, and had turned down several chances to run for governor. Shy and disarmingly humble (he told Arthur Morgan to "get a bigger man"),[24] Morgan concealed behind his rustic ways a clear vision of what needed to be done for Valley agriculture, and a definite idea of how to do it. He was a canny, powerful character who was to be the sole determinant of the course of TVA's farm program.

On the power issue, Morgan's chief complaint was the lackadaisical performance of the private tradition in rural electrification. Speaking at a regional meeting of the National Electric Light Association in 1927, he had surprised his audience by charging them with neglect of their clear social duty to farmers.[25] In the TVA, Morgan's role in the power program would be small, but crucial. In the inner politics of the three-man board of directors, he turned out to be the swing man. His support would eventually decide which wing of the public tradition, the moderate or the militant, would prevail.

The president's requirement for the third director was familiarity with the utility issue. The bitter and protracted confrontation between the public and private traditions made this third selection an extraordinarily sensitive and important decision.

Chairman Morgan investigated two candidates suggested by Roosevelt, but both seemed excessively hostile toward private companies. Hopeful of avoiding an unpleasant fight with the utilities, Morgan did not wish to descend to their level of legal subterfuge and propaganda. He wanted to set up TVA's yardstick in peace, await its results with scientific detachment, and in the meantime get on with TVA's larger mission, which he regarded as an integrated whole of which power was only one part. Roosevelt seemed to agree. In his public statements and in his early conferences with Morgan, he emphasized the broad social aspects of the TVA. His willingness to drop the two objectionable candidates suggested to Morgan "that my agreement with him on power policy was not casual, but had been defined in these specific cases."[26] Morgan's quest for the third director continued.

Other upholders of the public tradition were equally concerned about the board membership, not that the directors might be too hostile to the private companies but that they might be too friendly. Norris was skeptical in particular about Harcourt Morgan, whom rumor had connected with power companies in Tennessee. A hurried investigation by Norris himself proved the rumor groundless, but he still felt that the two Morgans, "while very conscientious and able, have never had the experience of fighting such opposition as is against them now." Judson King observed "several disturbing things about the behavior of Dr. [Arthur] Morgan," who told him, according to King, that he was "not going to fight the power companies."[27]

It was Justice Louis D. Brandeis who first suggested the name of the man Chairman Morgan selected as the third director. Brandeis's daughter, a resident of Madison, Wisconsin, had noted with admiration the work of young David E. Lilienthal, who had come to the state's Public Service Commission in 1931. Morgan's investigator found Lilienthal's local reputation to be extraordinary. Governor Philip La Follette called the commissioner his own best appointee and the best man he knew for the TVA directorship. Professor John R. Commons, who had set up the original commission for La Follette's father in 1907, declared that Lilienthal had "remade" it.

Only thirty-three years old, Lilienthal had grown up in Indiana, where his father, a Jewish immigrant from central Europe, operated retail stores in several towns in the northern part of the state. After a successful undergraduate career at DePauw University, David Lilienthal had entered Harvard Law School. Imbued with social conscience (he had spent his summers working in the Gary mills and other industrial plants), Lilienthal wanted to become a labor lawyer, and began in his first year at Harvard to make his presence known to persons who could help him. He introduced himself by letter to Professor Felix Frankfurter, wrote to such labor leaders as William Green and William Johnston, and carried on an extended correspondence with Frank P. Walsh, beginning a decade before Walsh's appointment by Roosevelt to the New York Power Authority.

"Confining my energies has always been an extremely trying piece of discipline for me," Lilienthal wrote in 1924. "I nearly killed myself in college, for instance, doing a multitude of things, all of which seemed of tremendous importance to me."[28] He was a terribly intense young man, ambitious and impatient to enter the contest between labor and capital.

Throughout his life—at Harvard, in Wisconsin, in the TVA, in the Atomic Energy Commission, and in private business—Lilienthal invested whatever he was doing with cosmic importance. Sometimes, as in the Atomic Energy Commission, this attitude was justified. But always it was a potent source of boundless energy and of a mental toughness that made him, on occasion, capable of harsh and merciless treatment of his enemies.

With the assistance of Frankfurter and Walsh, he became an associate, after graduation, of Donald Richberg, whose small Chicago firm specialized in labor law. Finding other outlets for his energies, Lilienthal wrote articles for several magazines, took part in the La Follette presidential campaign of 1924, and thought about teaching law as well as practicing. "Of course I am eager to be of whatever help I can," Frankfurter wrote him in 1924, "to your desire to teach labor law." But Lilienthal already had enough to do. The "multiplicity of your activities," as Frankfurter called it, had already caused some sloppy work in an important case argued by the Richberg firm before the Supreme Court. "I think your brief did not begin to scratch the surface," wrote Frankfurter. In it Lilienthal resorted to arguments "that do not hold water because they have been conclusively rejected by the court. . . . there is no excuse—except that you are trying to do too many things at the same time."[29]

After leaving Richberg's firm and setting up his own practice in Chicago, Lilienthal once served as co-counsel with Clarence Darrow in a criminal case, but steadily became more interested in public utility law, a sideline of Richberg and one of the fields Frankfurter taught at Harvard. In a famous rate suit in Chicago, he served as special counsel to the city, and helped win a dramatic refund of $20 million for customers of the telephone company. His law review articles gained the approval of such utility experts as James C. Bonbright of New York, and in a very few years after entering the field Lilienthal was a master of his subject.

At thirty-one he was the youngest appointee in the history of the Wisconsin Railroad Commission. Instructed by Governor La Follette, Lilienthal drafted legislation broadening the commission's powers and changing its name to Public Service Commission. He then set about his work, convinced of its crucial importance. In public speeches he reiterated again and again the central tenet of the public tradition: *"A public utility enterprise is a public business."*[30] His aggressive pursuit of the public interest attracted national attention in utility circles. At a convention of commissioners, disgusted at the bibulous fraternization with men representing the regulated interests, he staged a walkout.

"Probably no member of the new Commission was more outstanding than Commissioner Lilienthal," wrote a careful student of the Wisconsin agency, "although his accomplishments must be offset to a degree by the friction and animosity he created in the relations between the utilities and the Commission. . . . such an attitude is not completely helpful in the negotiational procedure which characterizes much of the regulatory process."[31]

To the utilities magnates Lilienthal had become anathema. As his term of appointment neared its end in 1933, the Wisconsin Telephone Company led a movement to get rid of him. Governor La Follette had failed to secure his party's renomination in 1932, and it was obvious that Lilienthal, after only two years' residence the center of a political controversy, might not be confirmed by the state senate even if he were reappointed by the new governor. The expected floor fight was averted only by his departure for Tennessee.

Milo Maltbie of the New York commission told Lilienthal in 1932 that if Governor Roosevelt won the presidential election, there would be a new Federal Utilities Commission and Lilienthal would be a member. Always ahead of events, Lilienthal began on his own to draft legislation for the new commission. Although the new commission never materialized, the TVA did, and it was no secret that he was being considered for one of the three directorships. Shortly after his preappointment interview with Arthur Morgan, Lilienthal told a newspaperman that the power companies, led by Commonwealth and Southern, were lobbying desperately to prevent the appointment of someone like himself; someone, as he said, who had "had intimate, rough and tumble contact with the power companies," unlike Chairman Arthur Morgan.[32]

To Tennessee David Lilienthal took a keen mind, a bold aggressiveness, an uncommon ambition, and a determination to uphold his idea of the public tradition against all challengers, outside the TVA and inside too. "Not often," Frankfurter wrote Roosevelt, "does one get such a combination of training, courage, understanding and youthful ardor as Lilienthal represents. It is a truly great appointment." The pairing of Arthur Morgan and Lilienthal was a master stroke. "That's a team," wrote Frankfurter, "that is bound to produce great results."[33] Some of the results of the pairing would have been hard to predict.

Of all the proponents of the public tradition, none was happier than George Norris over the appointment. For despite his youth, Lilienthal had one talent that would be invaluable in the coming fight with the utilities. "I do not believe it would be possible," wrote the senator, "for any scheme, however well disguised, to be put over on him."[34]

3 TVA VERSUS C & S

"I RECALL," Harcourt Morgan wrote years afterward, "our headquarters was like a mad house with telephones ringing, visitors, job seekers, Congressmen sponsoring certain friends, and news men." The board's first meeting formally incorporated the Tennessee Valley Authority on June 16, 1933, in the unlikely setting of a room at the Willard Hotel in Washington, where Arthur Morgan had set up a temporary headquarters. The meeting lasted eight hours, as the board plunged into its myriad business.[1]

Of special interest was a letter Chairman Morgan had received from Wendell L. Willkie, the new president of Commonwealth and Southern Corporation, the holding company with major interests in the Tennesse Valley. "It occurs to me," wrote Willkie, "that your new undertaking presents to both of us problems of mutual interest, the proper solution of which, for the good of all concerned, will require our early and continued cooperative efforts." The letter caused a long discussion over policy and strategy between Chairman Morgan and Director Lilienthal, with Harcourt Morgan playing the role of mediator. He would play the same role many more times in the discordant personal drama between his two colleagues which would run for five years. Arthur Morgan said TVA's relations with the power companies should be candid and forthright. Willkie's letter had asked for a meeting with Morgan, which the board authorized, cautioning the chairman against a premature commitment of the TVA to any specific policy.[2]

At forty-one Wendell Willkie was the youngest head of any large utility system. For several reasons he was precisely the man to undertake the task of rebuilding the private tradition's reputation, then at its nadir. A Wilsonian Democrat, Willkie contrasted sharply with the reactionaries who had dominated the industry in the 1920s and remained high in its councils.[3]

All four of Willkie's grandparents had emigrated from Germany. He himself had grown up in Elwood, Indiana, a small boom town in which his parents, a remarkable pair, both practiced law and sometimes taught school. As a boy he was prankish, aggressive, and clumsy. His academic career was undistinguished, but like David Lilienthal he demonstrated as early as high school an extraordinary talent for debate and public speaking. His undergraduate years at Indiana University were later dramatized by publicists who had him chewing tobacco, wearing a red turtle-neck sweater, spouting socialist ideas, and vituperating against the fraternity system and the law faculty.[4] Actually Willkie was not at all the campus radical. He presided over two school spirit committees, and as a member of the student Democratic Club began his life-long support of the ideas of Woodrow Wilson, then the progressive governor of New Jersey.

After graduation Willkie earned money for law school as a high school teacher. He also worked briefly as a chemist in a Puerto Rican sugar plant, where he witnessed episodes of brutality that helped to keep him, as he later told a journalist, from thinking like the typical American millionaire. A much more conscientious student when he returned to Bloomington, he won every scholastic prize in the law school. His address as class orator, entitled "The New Freedom" after Wilson's recent book, denounced Indiana's constitution and proposed a new one patterned after Wilsonian regulation of business and banking. When the United States entered the war, he enlisted, was quickly commissioned a first lieutenant, and reached France a short time before Armistice Day. At twenty-seven he returned to Indiana, ready to begin his legal career.

Willkie now had ambitions Elwood could never satisfy. His application to the Firestone company of Akron, Ohio, mentioned his "conviction that the future of a lawyer in a town of 10,000 is very much limited."[5] Akron, by contrast, was an excellent place for a young lawyer to get ahead. Its new industries, based on the automobile boom, had sent the city's population from less than 70,000 in 1910 to more than 200,000 by 1920. His job at Firestone Tire and Rubber was to furnish free legal aid to employees, at a salary of $2500 a year. Like Franklin D. Roosevelt, Willkie speculated during the twenties in stocks and real estate, with mixed success.

He left Firestone in 1921 to join the small but prosperous firm of Mather and Nesbitt, whose clients included some of the region's richest corporations: Ohio State Bank and Trust, the Erie Railroad, and most important for his future, Northern Ohio Traction and Light (later Ohio Edison), one of the 165 companies which became part of the far-flung Commonwealth and Southern system. With his zeal for work, his competitive instinct, and his exceptional ability to speak extemporaneously, Willkie soon became the firm's best trial lawyer. Some years he was in court two hundred days. Ideally suited for his job, Willkie was a hard man to dislike, and his passion for victory was somehow inoffensive, even though some of his clients were not.

As protected monopolies, most utilities are inherently suspect to both customers and juries. Willkie often represented the power company in negotiations for franchise renewals, and he defended numerous personal injury suits resulting from collisions of streetcars and pedestrians, in which the maimed plaintiff elected the jury's natural sympathies. He had other clients too, later estimating that only a fourth of his practice and income derived from utility work, and "had nothing whatsoever to do with legislative or Congressional matters."[6] But the power company was deeply involved in politics, and so was Willkie himself.

A lieutenant of Newton D. Baker, he went as a delegate to the Democratic National Convention of 1924. In the famous acrimony of that convention he worked for Smith's nomination and for strong planks endorsing the League of Nations and denouncing the Ku Klux Klan. Willkie's efforts for both these planks reflected commitments that would stay with him the rest of his life. His defense of civil rights often won high praise, and his internationalism would be one important basis for the bipartisan American foreign policy which emerged in the 1940s. Baker, who after leaving Wilson's Cabinet had set up a law practice in Cleveland, markedly influenced Willkie's thoughts on foreign affairs. In the 1930s he also helped the utility companies fight their legal battles against the New Deal.

In October 1929, just before the Great Crash, Willkie took the giant step from Akron to New York. Bernard C. Cobb, the prime mover in the formation of the new Commonwealth and Southern Corporation, tapped him to be one of the company's legal advisers, at an annual salary of $36,000. In three years Willkie would assume C & S's presidency, at $75,000.

Commonwealth and Southern, one of the last utility-holding companies to sprout from the consolidation movement, was — contrary to the pattern — one of the best. By mid-1933, Cobb and Willkie had eliminated all upstream loans, intermediate holding companies, and service affiliates designed to bleed profits from helpless operating subsidiaries. Although C & S began life with a heavy burden of watered stock (the capitalization of the constituent companies being approximately doubled in the process of combination), the water was squeezed out by 1933 in a rigorous write-down. But additional overcapitalization, of uncertain origin and amount, inhered in the operating companies, and would cause acute valuation problems, both for ratemaking and for future sales of property to the TVA. Still, C & S was an excellent business organization. James C. Bonbright, the Columbia economist who served on Governor Roosevelt's Power Authority, called it in 1932 the "best managed of the utility holding companies."[7]

It was a vast operation. Of C & S's thirteen major subsidiaries, eleven were primarily electric utilities: Consumers Power (Michigan), Central Illinois Light, Southern Indiana Gas and Electric, Ohio Edison, Pennsylvania Power, Tennessee Electric Power, Alabama Power, Georgia Power, Gulf Power (Florida), Mississippi Power, and South Carolina Power. C & S owned virtually all the common stock of these companies, and some of the preferred. By 1933 the group's total assets amounted to well over a billion dollars, with annual revenues in excess of $100 million, of which 80 percent derived from electricity. The constituent companies provided service measured by over a million meters in 2677 communities with a total population just over five million. It was one of the largest of all public utility holding companies, and its history of repeated mergers into ever larger groups followed the pattern of the industry during the twenties, when nearly four thousand companies merged into consolidated firms.[8]

The southern group of the new company, comprising mainly the Alabama, Tennessee, and Georgia subsidiaries, was about equal in assets to the northern group. Because of the TVA, it was much more of a headache politically, and partly as a result of the political problem, economically too. The elevation of such a man as Willkie — an unusual combination of shrewd attorney and public relations man — could not have been unrelated to the anticipated trouble with the New Deal in the Tennessee Valley.[9]

In the years ahead Willkie's role would be what it had been in Akron — advocate, special pleader. As in Akron, Willkie himself would seem to his audience somehow better than his client, somehow free of the tarnish with which the industry had covered itself. In him the private tradition had found an articulate salesman possessed of genuine conviction, formidable negotiating ability, and an amazing knack for making old arguments sound new and appealing.

Willkie's unbroken success within the economy of big business militated against any revulsion from it. Committed to getting ahead — as his wife once remarked, he did not want to have to ask the price of something he wanted to buy — he had wholeheartedly entered the chase after power, fame, and money.[10] His own experience seemed to testify that the American system offered an abundance of all three to a man of sufficient talent. Accordingly, whatever reformism he felt was oriented entirely to improvements of the existing economic system. His addresses before service clubs in Akron, where he was a popular speaker, reflected these convictions; his themes were defense of the League of Nations, the power industry, and the freedom of the American economy, and attacks on the Klan and the idea of war. Though Willkie admitted the need for some regulation of utilities, he did not regard the C & S electric business as essentially different from the Firestone rubber business. In effect he rejected the public tradition's idea of a utility as something peculiarly apart, a creature of the political state. To him the Electric Age was the child of a single parent — private enterprise.

A big, well-read, quick-thinking, supremely self-confident man, Willkie ideally fitted his new job. He had none of the city slicker in him. Like Benjamin Franklin at Paris, he affected a rusticity not entirely genuine, using his shuffling gait, rumpled attire, and Hoosier speech (he said "pahr" for power), to charm reporters, investors, and congressmen. He bore as little resemblance to Insull as Roosevelt did to Harding.

Sixty days after Willkie took the helm of C & S, Roosevelt became president of the United States. Willkie had favored Smith or Baker for the nomination, but he voted for Roosevelt and contributed $150 to the campaign fund.

Willkie met Arthur Morgan in a private dining room at the University Club in New York on the evening of June 28, 1933. At issue was where and what the TVA yardstick would be. The title of the Tennessee Valley Authority Act, though it mentioned such functions as reforestation and the proper use of marginal lands, for some reason contained no reference to electric power. The word "yardstick" appeared nowhere in the text. Throughout, the power program yielded primacy to TVA's responsibilities in flood control and channel improvement, the constitutional props supporting the entire program. The operations of the TVA were not limited to the Tennessee drainage basin, but included its "adjoining territory," a hopelessly ambiguous term. TVA could distribute its power to customers "within transmission distance," another vague phrase. Transmission distance of electricity was at the time variously estimated as between two hundred and three hundred miles. Thus TVA could reach, from hydro sites along the Tennessee and its tributaries, such cities as Pittsburgh, St. Louis, and Atlanta, and practically the entire area served by Willkie's southern companies. The Authority was in a powerful legal position to acquire a vast territory for its yardstick.[11]

Excepting the yardstick, the Act did define the general aims of the power program. It directed the Authority "to promote and encourage the fullest possible use of electric light and power on farms"; it cautioned against duplication of existing power facilities; it permitted TVA to prescribe retail rates at which its power would be sold to the consumer by intermediate public or private agencies (TVA's policy was not to sell power to residential customers at retail but to intermediate marketers); and most important of all, it mandated a preference in power sales for public agencies — mainly nonprofit municipal and cooperative distributors.

Aside from its application to cooperatives, the preference clause was not new in the TVA Act. It had been settled policy for most federal hydro dams since 1906. But historically the clause had been administered in different ways, and the idea itself was open to several interpretations. Administrators could construe it loosely, to mean preference at a given time, on a first-come first-served basis, or over a long, even indefinite period.[12] The clause had already engendered bitter controversies (notably in the case of the Hetch-Hetchy project near San Francisco), and would remain a serious problem of public policy long after the New Deal. For the TVA, the preference clause would be a source of unending friction with Commonwealth and Southern, and even within the TVA board itself.

The discussion in New York between Morgan and Willkie was friendly enough, but the two men could not agree on the meaning of these provisions of the TVA Act and on their effect in Willkie's southern territory. Besides a mutual concurrence that, as Morgan wrote in a memorandum to his colleagues, "we could get along best if we could each depend on the other as being direct and straightforward," the meeting accomplished little.[13]

One reason was that whereas Willkie had complete charge of the negotiations on the private side (indeed as surrogate for the entire private tradition, which watched the evolution of the TVA with well-founded horror that Roosevelt might try to duplicate it elsewhere), the public side was represented inside the TVA by two conflicting viewpoints. As far as the TVA itself was concerned, the militant viewpoint prevailed, owing to an alliance of David Lilienthal with Harcourt Morgan, which in effect gave the agriculturist direct administrative responsibility for the farm program in return for his support of Lilienthal's administration and policies in the power program.[14] But for a time, Lilienthal's militancy was circumscribed by the influence of President Roosevelt, who in the early months of TVA tended to support the moderate viewpoint of Arthur Morgan.

Chairman Morgan regarded the power issue as an apolitical problem of economics and engineering. Thoroughly committed to the yardstick idea, he wanted to negotiate the peaceful transfer of a representative rural-urban area from

Willkie's companies to the TVA. After this transfer there
would be no direct competition for customers and no propaganda by either side. The yardstick experiment would be
scientific, with accounting methods designed to afford fair
comparisons with operations of private companies. A panel
of impartial economists would evaluate and announce the
results of the experiment, and their verdict would guide
public policy. Morgan did not want TVA's other missions
endangered by political agitation over the explosive public
power question, and he believed negotiations with Willkie
should begin immediately. He knew the insidious side of
the private tradition's history, yet he had no fear of Willkie.
He believed that the government's superior resources and
powers implied a special responsibility to be fair to private
companies.[15]

Morgan's arguments reflected a supreme confidence in
the institutional superiority of the government, but an unfortunate lack of familiarity with the vocabulary of public
utility accounting. His facile use and implied acceptance,
for example, of such terms as "going value" and "reproduc-
tion cost," two of the power companies' favorite devices for
inflating the value of their properties, suggested to Lilienthal and other fierce upholders of the public tradition that
Morgan was either allied with the enemy or hopelessly naive,
and therefore dangerous. Both assessments missed the mark.
Morgan was simply very confident and full of good will,
quite ready to give Willkie a chance to redeem the private
tradition.[16]

The need of a market for Wilson Dam power made the
yardstick an immediate problem. Several municipalities had
applied to TVA for service and were insistently pressing
their requests in competition with each other. A few had
local publicly owned distribution systems, but most were
being served by Commonwealth and Southern or other
private companies. For Lilienthal the obvious course was
to ignore Willkie for the time being. This would permit
TVA to gather the technical information necessary for fitting

its supply to its customers' demands. The Authority would then set up wholesale and retail rate schedules, and deal with the impatient municipalities individually.

Thinking of the immediate interests of the consumer (and of his own strategy regarding Willkie), Lilienthal envisioned not one large yardstick area, but several small spots, which would serve more as a potent political spur to regulation than as a scientific proving ground. For the moment TVA's only source of power was Wilson Dam, whose limited output would have stronger impact in yardstick islands than in one large area. Besides the delays involved in acquiring such an area, he doubted that Willkie would sell at a fair price, owing to what Lilienthal regarded as excessive property valuations. His lack of solicitude for Willkie was rooted in his recognition of the private tradition's unmitigated hostility to public power and in his conviction, derived from his experience in Wisconsin, that power magnates could not be trusted, irrespective of the friendly and cooperative attitude assumed by Willkie himself. The government might be institutionally superior to private companies in the abstract, but Lilienthal had seen as a state commissioner how the utilities played the judiciary off against the other branches of government to thwart the public interest.

Most important of all, Lilienthal had none of Morgan's reluctance to enter into political agitation and propaganda. Indeed he welcomed the opportunity. In the first place, he regarded the power question as fundamentally political, not economic or technical. Essential to any real progress was political education of the public, and voters who quickly forgot a sterile economic pronouncement would vividly remember a partisan fight. Second, wide and constant publicity was necessary to induce the public to increase its consumption of electricity and therefore permit lower rates (owing to the sharply declining costs of production and distribution as consumption increased). Lilienthal appreciated Morgan's desire to treat Willkie and his investors fairly. "But to premise our power policy at this time," he informed the chairman, "on the willingness of the privately owned utilities to work with us, seems to me to be running counter to every reasonable expectation under the circumstances, and what is vastly more important, to expose the work of the Authority to the gravest hazards."[17] Willkie could wait, as Norris had waited throughout the twenties. In the meantime there were more important matters to settle. The first was to formulate and publish a TVA power policy; the second to set wholesale and retail rates for TVA's electricity.

The enunciation of a power policy originated in Arthur Morgan's complaint that TVA had no coherent policy but was unavoidably creating one in its negotiations with municipalities.[18] Unable to agree on the matter of "territorial restriction" — whether or not to entertain applications for service from public agencies within transmission distance but outside the selected yardstick areas — Morgan and Lilienthal took the matter to the president.

After the White House conference the two directors went to Morgan's room at the nearby Cosmos Club, where Lilienthal presented and Morgan, after certain changes, approved a comprehensive policy statement for release to the press. A very important document, the "power policy" release was a detailed eleven-point outline of TVA's plans.[19] The basic disagreement over territorial restriction was resolved in points seven and eight, according to a compromise suggested in part by Roosevelt.

Point one explicitly declared the public tradition's fundamental dogma about the nature of a public utility: "The business of generating and distributing electric power is a public business." Points two, three, four, and six affirmed the superiority of the public to the private interest, calling for a reconciliation of the two where possible. Point five, derived from Roosevelt's Portland speech, asserted the right of communities to own and operate their electric systems. "Such a course of action may take the form of acquiring the existing plant or setting up a competing plant, as circumstances may dictate."

It omitted the controversial phrase about a punitive "birch rod in the cupboard" contained in both the Portland speech and Lilienthal's first draft.

Points seven and eight, altered and amplified from Lilienthal's draft, resolved the basic question at issue and disclosed TVA's yardstick plans in some detail. Where the first draft rejected any "blanket agreement for division of territory with private utilities" and posited a piecemeal approach, the final version represented a meeting of minds among Morgan, Lilienthal, and Roosevelt: "To provide a workable and economic basic of operations, the Authority plans initially to serve certain definite regions and to develop its program in those areas before going outside." The areas lay in the strip "immediately proximate" to the transmission line the TVA intended to build between Wilson Dam in Alabama and the projected Norris Dam (named for the senator) in eastern Tennessee; the region around Muscle Shoals, including northern Alabama and northeastern Mississippi; and the territory around Norris Dam, whose completion in about three years would provide another source of power. The eventual yardstick would encompass, roughly, the state of Tennessee and the Tennessee River watershed lying in small parts of other states. It would include at least one city, such as Birmingham, Memphis, Louisville, or Atlanta, whose population exceeded a quarter of a million. "Where special considerations exist, justifying the Authority's going outside this initial area, the Authority will receive and consider applications based on such special considerations . . . [as] unreasonably high rates for service and a failure . . . to protect the public interest."

Points nine, ten, and eleven stipulated that the TVA would try to avoid wasteful duplication of and competition with private facilities, keep its accounts so as to show a fair yardstick of "comparision of operations with privately owned plants," and open the accounts to inspection by the public.

For a press release, the power policy was a puissant and candid statement, a bold and direct threat to the private tradition. Still, it was ambiguous enough to allow policies ranging from thorough cooperation with Willkie's companies to outright and total war.[20] The private tradition's own course of action would partly determine which policy would prevail. For the moment, it was not clear precisely what TVA would do next. The government still held the initiative, as Lilienthal wished, and Willkie remained off balance.

With the power policy set, the next task was to establish a rate schedule for TVA electricity. Under the best circumstances, rate making is a difficult undertaking. For the TVA it was highly speculative as well, because the Authority had no clear idea of its costs or of its market. Yet rates had to be set quickly. TVA needed figures to show the impatient municipalities clamoring to hook up to its power lines. The problem was fundamentally one of accounting, but the resolution would have powerful political reverberations. The extremely low rates which emerged from the Authority's calculations would be the primary weapon in TVA's battle for public opinion, and the primary target of the private tradition's counter-propaganda. The marriage of low rates with the yardstick idea created a major public controversy.

TVA's chief electrical engineer was Llewellyn Evans, former manager of the public power system in Tacoma, Washington. Possessing an almost metaphysical belief in low-cost, high-usage economics, Evans also wanted to reverse the private tradition's policy of giving every advantage to large consumers. Though all utilities, publicly or privately owned, needed large customers, Evans believed in minimizing the price advantages given to industrial firms, and maximizing those given to householders. He was, as TVA's former general counsel Joseph Swidler remarked many years later, "a prophet and a visionary."[21] Perhaps more than any other person, Evans shaped the contours of TVA's rate structure.

One of the first steps in making the rates was to set a valuation for the source of power, Wilson Dam. The dam had been constructed with frequent interruptions in a period of high prices, had other purposes besides power, and had depreciated in the years since its completion. The valuation, though vital to the rates finally set, would be essentially arbitrary. The dam had cost about $48 million, of which one-fourth was for navigation facilities. Working with the remainder, Lilienthal, Evans, and their several consultants[22] arrived at an adjusted and depreciated figure of about $24 million. This amount happily coincided with a figure calculated from multiplying a desirable installed-kilowatt figure for well-planned hydro dams ($125, revised upward from $100 at Arthur Morgan's request for conservative computations), by the hydro potential of the dam (195,000 kilowatts), which yields $24,375,000. This figure, with adjustments for the small government steam plant near the dam and other minor factors, was TVA's initial rate base.

The next step was to calculate or guess at the market potential and the expected customer demand. Here the patterns were Ontario Hydro, the Tacoma and Seattle municipal plant, and two municipal systems in Wisconsin. In an extremely bold decision, one of the boldest TVA ever made, the group hypothesized an average annual consumption by residential customers of 1200 kilowatt-hours. At the time the average consumption in the United States was 595. In Willkie's nearby companies it was 612 for Tennessee Electric Power, 803 for Georgia Power, and 793 for Alabama Power.[23] In effect, TVA was flatly predicting that its low rates would cause an increase in consumption of between 50 and 100 percent. The rates themselves, avowedly promotional, were based on such an increase, and would prove economically sound only if the increase occurred.

The ratemakers disagreed among themselves over many details, but they all knew that prices had to be set quickly. They accordingly took short cuts, employed arbitrary figures and methods, and finished their work in a ridiculously brief time. Most of the consultants were highly qualified economists, but their work in this case was basically (and necessarily) an exercise in intuition.

For a utility rate structure, the results were exceptionally simple and easy to understand, well suited for use in publicity. Indeed Lilienthal published them before submitting them for formal board approval. In a press release of September 14, 1933, referring somewhat disingenuously to "weeks of careful study of costs and market factors," he outlined a price scale which would result in electric bills "for the typical general consumer . . . of about 2 cents a kilowatt hour, and for the typical limited user an average of about 2¾ cents. For a fully electrified home—which is our objective—the rate would average 7 mills per kilowatt hour." At the time the national average was about 5.5 cents; for the customers of Tennessee Electric Power, 5.8 cents; of Alabama Power, 4.6 cents; of Georgia Power, 5.2 cents.[24]

TVA issued a second press release the next day declaring that "all costs of service are included, and, in addition, provision has been made for items of cost not actually incurred, such as taxes and interest, but which were nevertheless included in order to make fair comparison with privately operated utilities, for 'yardstick' purposes."[25] At best this statement was misleading. Ultimately Lilienthal would have to qualify some of his yardstick claims, but for the moment his intention was clear. He was challenging the private tradition to match TVA's rates, and insisting by the yardstick implication that it could be done. TVA's rate levels represented a gigantic gamble that price elasticity of demand was drastically greater than private operators had believed. And Lilienthal had a plan to insure that the gamble paid off.

He traced the outlines of his plan in a confidential letter to the White House:

> The private utilities had substantially all the market in our area, and have installed capactiy [sic] approximately 30% in excess of the present requirements of that market. The only way we could get the "yardstick" operating was to take away their market. This would greatly increase their unused facilities. Confronted by this problem, we sought to devise some means

of increasing the demand for electricity so as to make room for the existing systems as well as the system which we are creating. We concluded that this can only be done by large-scale distribution of appliances, and the lowering of rates.

Lilienthal hoped that the program could be applied eventually on a national scale, to break the business logjam of high rates for electricity and high prices for appliances. With high rates, appliances were too expensive to operate; with high appliance prices, many consumers could not afford to buy them and thereby use more electricity. To help the campaign Lilienthal envisioned a "public relations angle" stimulated by "the dramatic effect of a statement by the President on the 'Electrification of America.'" Social gains would be twofold: increased employment in the appliance manufacturing industry and lower utility rates throughout the country.[26]

TVA at once set up the plan in the Tennessee Valley through a consumer credit affiliate called the Electric Home and Farm Authority, which granted low-interest loans for appliance purchases and worked with manufacturers to get low-cost appliances onto the market. Lilienthal planned to invite Willkie's companies to participate. The increased usage by their customers would soften the blow of TVA's expropriation of a yardstick market.

After his initial meeting with Arthur Morgan, Willkie had no personal contacts with the TVA board for the next three months, aside from a few unimportant exchanges of letters. Lilienthal, willing to allow his adversary to grow worried and impatient, had put off Willkie's requests for a conference until TVA established its power policy and rate schedules. He had opposed broad negotiations and had been emphatically supported in this view by such public power advocates outside the TVA as Senators Norris and La Follette, Morris L. Cooke, and Felix Frankfurter, all of whom he consulted during his early disagreement with Chairman Morgan.[27]

The question of some sort of settlement, however, was now becoming inescapable. Willkie, after all, was TVA's number one customer. A War Department contract dating originally from 1925 provided for the sale of Wilson Dam electricity to the Alabama Power Company. The contract would expire on January 1, 1934. Without a renewal TVA stood to lose substantial and badly needed income, since it had just begun to negotiate with other customers, most of whom represented only small markets.[28] This queer customer-enemy status of Commonwealth and Southern imposed a basic paradox on the relationship between Lilienthal and Willkie, and caused TVA trouble for several years.

Besides straightening out the Wilson Dam question, Lilienthal wished to secure Willkie's cooperation in the appliance sales program he had outlined for the president. And if TVA was to set up its yardstick without duplicating private facilities, as the power policy implied, Willkie had to be consulted. His companies served most of the prospective yardstick market.

In what was to be the first one of scores of conferences over the next six years, Willkie and Lilienthal met on October 4, 1933, at the Cosmos Club in Washington. "I recall," wrote Lilienthal several years afterward, "that we were two exceedingly cagey fellows who met at lunch that noon." Willkie, having had a long time to think over his strategy, went boldly on the offensive with a specific proposal. His companies would buy all of TVA's electricity. The New Deal, he argued, was a passing fancy, and TVA depended on appropriations from a Congress which might at any moment reverse its present mood of generosity. Accordingly, TVA should sell Willkie its power, for about a half-million dollars a year, and become "independent of Congress." There was no need to expend a lot of energy looking for a public market. "This proposition didn't evoke any enthusiasm on my part, to put it mildly," Lilienthal recalled, "but I didn't say anything about it, being somewhat overwhelmed by his cocksureness." The first meeting ended inconclusively. Though "pretty badly scared," Lilienthal made no commitment, and reported the conference to the board.[29]

Before the next important meeting TVA completed a preliminary agreement with the town of Tupelo, Mississippi, to begin wholesale service by February 1934. Tupelo was the home of Congressman John Rankin, who had sponsored the Norris TVA bill in the House and was, next to Norris, TVA's best friend in Congress. The town owned a public distribution system, and therefore could negotiate immediately with TVA. The acquisition of this customer materially enhanced Lilienthal's position with Willkie. It provided TVA with at least one yardstick area, however tiny, and showed that the Authority's power program was going forward with or without Willkie's cooperation.[30] In the ensuing months the little town of Tupelo would become famous as a synonym for "yardstick," and would be the focus of propaganda barrages from both sides.

Weeks of difficult infighting among Willkie, Lilienthal, and their staffs followed the Tupelo agreement.[31] Willkie spoke histrionically of fighting fire with fire, forced betrayal of his stockholders, and large severance damages. Above all he wanted to prevent TVA from building a transmission line from Muscle Shoals to Norris Dam, through the heart of the Tennessee Electric Power Company's market. At one point he offered to sell the whole company to TVA as an alternative. But the company had a book value of $100 million, and an outright purchase appeared too big a step to take so early— partly because it would require additional legislation, and partly because the actual properties were not worth $100 million. Instead, TVA went ahead with building its transmission line.

The Willkie-Lilienthal relationship was one of extreme mutual wariness and respect, which increased as the negotiations continued. The two men agreed on the load-building appliance program, on the general principle of a rate reduction by the Tennessee Electric Power Company (TEPCO), and on the obvious fact that TVA was going into the power business. The stumbling block was the extent of territory TVA would receive for its yardstick. The negotiations deadlocked on this issue for almost two months, until the War

Department contract had only two weeks to run.

In an ultimatum, Lilienthal now proposed that TVA be ceded certain named counties in Alabama, Mississippi, and Tennessee, and the transmission lines to reach them. "This proposition was coupled with the statement," Lilienthal reported to the board, "that if the C and S did not desire to sell these transmission facilities or the prices which it placed on them were, in the judgment of the Board of Directors, unreasonable, then the Authority would proceed to build duplicate transmission facilities in the area."

This threat put heavy pressure on Willkie. If he rejected the proposal he risked losing part of the market anyway, for several towns had already voted to convert to public power and ally with TVA. And some of these municipalities were availing themselves of loans and grants from the Public Works Administration to build their own public distribution systems. PWA's role in the Roosevelt administration's recovery program had surpassing importance for the power fight. It multiplied the pressure on Willkie, and he decided to accept Lilienthal's proposition. Within three weeks the two men had worked out all details, and on January 4, 1934, they incorporated their agreement into a formal contract.

Willkie agreed to continue his option to purchase wholesale power from Wilson Dam, the sale being cancellable by TVA. He contracted to sell specific systems in northeastern Mississippi to the TVA for $850,000; and options on properties in northern Alabama and eastern Tennessee, the price on transfer being $1 million paid to the Alabama Power Company and $900,000 to TEPCO. All parties would cooperate in the promotion of appliance sales, and TEPCO agreed to make a domestic rate reduction totalling $415,000 annually. Commonwealth and Southern could not sell electricity within the "ceded area," and TVA must forego further incursions into the private companies' markets. The contract would last for five years or until Norris Dam began producing power, whichever came first.[32]

The settlement contained significant concessions by both

sides. For Willkie, the mere fact of relinquishing some of his territory voluntarily (though under manifold pressures), formally acknowledged TVA's right to enter the power business, in an area understood to serve as a yardstick. For Lilienthal, the prohibition on TVA's going outside this area for customers conceded a point not only to Willkie, but to Chairman Arthur Morgan. Originally Lilienthal had flatly refused to make such a commitment, which apparently violated TVA's announced power policy as well as the preference clause in the TVA Act. Norris, the author of the bill, had declared emphatically that such an agreement, besides being "unnecessary" and beneficial only to "the power trust," was a "violation of existing law," since it went counter to the preference clause.[33]

But Norris was mistaken. The law could be interpreted in several ways. Lilienthal's interpretation, which pressures from Morgan and Roosevelt forced him to make, demonstrated the flexibility of the preference clause as an administrative tool capable of serving different goals. When fully served, the ceded areas contained sufficient demand to absorb all the power TVA had available. If the hypothetical problem arose — if public agencies outside the ceded areas applied for TVA service — the Authority could reply with the simple argument that it had no electricity to sell. During the life of the January 4 contract, TVA would negotiate with municipalities and cooperatives within the ceded areas on an individual basis, until all its power was obligated to these public agencies. In the meantime, Willkie would buy TVA power for his companies, in ever diminishing amounts, and the Authority would continue to receive needed revenues.

There appeared, then, no obstacle to peace between TVA and C & S. Compromise and cooperation, at arms-length bargaining sessions, seemed to have settled the issue for the good of all concerned. January 4, 1934, marked the high point in good feeling between the public and private traditions in the Tennessee Valley.

4

POLARIZATION

THE JANUARY 4 CONTRACT, by providing at least a temporary basis for cooperation between TVA and Commonwealth and Southern, held out hope that the public and private traditions might avoid full-scale conflict in the Tennessee Valley. This hope failed, because the terms of the contract were not met, and also because the differences between TVA and C & S were only a part of the clash between the objectives of the New Deal and the interests of the privately owned utilities. The contract provided a respite from direct competition for markets, but both sides used the respite to marshal their forces for further battle. The animosity between TVA and C & S was higher when the contract expired than when it began.

Foremost among the benefits TVA hoped to secure from the contract was a functioning yardstick market area which would demonstrate incontestably to the nation the virtues of public power. That the yardstick dream did not come true was partly owing to flaws in the idea itself, but the first obstacle to its realization came from Commonwealth and Southern. The January 4 contract provided that TVA would receive from C & S certain properties in Mississippi, Alabama, and Tennessee. The company delivered the Mississippi properties on June 1, 1934, and TVA began its yardstick operations there.[1] With the Alabama and Tennessee properties, a complex of difficulties intervened, and the good will symbolized by the contract began to dissipate.

67

TVA was to buy from the Alabama Power Company the transmission lines reaching out to certain cities, while the cities themselves purchased the company's local distribution facilities, for operation as public municipal systems. The sale of distribution systems would follow the company's agreement "with any such municipality on the price to be paid for the same. Alabama Company agrees to make every reasonable effort to come to an early agreement with said municipalities for such sales."[2]

According to an investigation by Joseph C. Swidler, a young TVA lawyer who handled the Authority's early acquisitions, what actually happened was that "all conferences opened with the statement that the company must have cash and would not consider bonds under any circumstances." For the small cities involved, indeed for small cities throughout the United States at this stage of the depression, a large cash payment for anything was practically impossible. If bonds were not acceptable, then they simply could not pay. Furthermore, the company demanded full book value for the properties, although its price to TVA for the transmission lines was only 60 percent of book value. In short, reported Swidler, there was "no room for doubt that the Alabama Power Company has made no genuine effort to comply with its contractual obligations to us."[3]

Lilienthal immediately protested to Willkie. Since TVA's honest efforts had encountered "a stone wall," he had no choice except to "do whatever I can to assist these communities in carrying their program forward by the alternative method of securing funds from the Public Works Administration." If the cities in the yardstick area could not pay the power company's prices for existing facilities, they could perhaps obtain money from PWA to build new, duplicate facilities.[4]

Willkie had signed the January 4 contract primarily to avoid just this kind of TVA-PWA pressure. His reply to Lilienthal was therefore conciliatory. Since the contract had been successful with this one exception, "it is my thought that there should be no impasse recognized until after we have an opportunity for full discussion." Lilienthal then proposed that TVA itself purchase the distribution systems, for a price lower than the company had offered the municipalities, then resell the property to the cities. Willkie had his doubts. "If I offered to sell for a lower price," he declared, "I would feel that I was but paying an additional amount to one agency of the Federal Government in order to eliminate the action of another Federal Agency [the Public Works Administration] in loaning money to duplicate and destroy the value of the property under discussion." After much haggling, however, the two men came to an agreement. In August, 1934, TVA's board of directors authorized purchase at the negotiated price. Two months later, the Alabama Public Service Commission having approved the sale, TVA tendered payment.[5]

But this plan also fell through. The company refused to turn over the property. The Chemical Bank and Trust Company of New York, which held a mortgage trusteeship on part of the sale property, refused to relinquish its lien, demanding either an independent appraisal or a deposit with the bank by TVA of a cash indemnity. This delay apparently violated the January 4 contract, in which Willkie had covenanted "to secure any necessary waiver of liens or encumbrances" on the property. The result of the delay, along with subsequent litigation, was that none of the Alabama properties actually changed hands until 1936, and even then only two of the fourteen systems involved. TVA encountered similar difficulties with C & S's Tennessee properties. When the Authority attempted to execute its option to buy, under the January 4 contract, the company replied that the transfer could not occur until settlement of the pending Alabama litigation.[6]

Concurrently with its dealings with C & S, TVA negotiated with a second giant holding company, Electric Bond and Share, for the purchase of other systems in Tennessee. An

Electric Bond and Share subsidiary served the attractive urban market of Knoxville, and another the even more lucrative one of Memphis. Here too, despite city referenda in favor of public power, a series of barriers — litigation and price — prevented peaceful transfers.[7]

For many months, therefore, TVA's market area consisted of a few spots in Mississippi and tiny parts of Alabama unaffected by the failure of the January 4 contract. With such a small territory in which to work, TVA could not hope to realize its great expectations for the yardstick.

For propaganda purposes, however, Tupelo and the other small communities sufficed nicely, and Lilienthal's speeches and press releases made the most of the area TVA did have. When, on a tour of the Valley in the fall of 1934, President Roosevelt rashly declared to the citizens of Tupelo that "what you are doing here is going to be copied in every State of the Union before we get through," he touched off a national debate over the yardstick. The debate quickly revealed grievous flaws in the idea itself, and that instead of a simple notion like Roosevelt's 1914 plan for the Navy's armor-plate, the electricity yardstick was a very confusing problem indeed.[8]

Several economic facts made it difficult to draw useful comparisons between TVA and private companies. Power operations in the private tradition were unified; a single company generated, transmitted, and distributed electricity. In the TVA, generation was by the federal government, transmission in the early months was over C & S lines (under a common use provision of the January 4 contract), and distribution was by municipal and cooperative public agencies. TVA had broken up the integrity of the power business as conducted in the private tradition, essentially by dividing the wholesale from the retail business. This fact alone tended to invalidate the deceptively simple rate comparisons made by TVA spokesmen.

And there were other reasons why such comparisons were

of dubious logic. TVA constructed its dams differently from the way a power company would build a single-purpose hydro dam. The Authority was the first important fruition of the progressive conservationists' idea of multiple-purpose river development. It was to be an exemplar of what rational planning could accomplish in flood control, river transportation, and hydroelectricity. TVA therefore designed its dams deliberately to maximize the benefits from all three. In order to establish a rate base for TVA electricity, it was necessary to apportion the cost of the dams among navigation, flood control, and power. TVA spent years on this allocation problem, and did not develop its final formula until 1937-38. Devised chiefly by the University of Wisconsin economist Martin G. Glaeser, the formula was as sound a method as could be conceived. But any method—indeed the very step of allocation—vitiated the use of TVA's dams as cost yardsticks. Furthermore, the multipurpose nature of the dams affected their methods of operation as well as accounting. At any given time, for example, the level of water ideal for flood control or navigation might differ from the optimum level for hydroelectric production. Since power was subordinated to the other functions, which provided TVA's constitutionality, the Authority sometimes controlled its dams so as to reduce their power potential.

Even the fact that TVA based its power operations exclusively on hydroelectricity made them ill-suited for use as a national yardstick. River systems of great hydro potential existed outside the Tennessee Valley, notably in the West and in the state of New York. But in most parts of the country coal-burning steam plants provided the cheapest method of producing electricity. Since the constitutional basis of the federal government's early power operations was its right to control waterways, any government power plant must be hydroelectric and therefore atypical. As Benjamin Cohen remarked privately in 1937, the notion of a yardstick for wholesale power production simply did not make good sense. "I think," said Cohen, "the sooner we explode it, the better."[9]

But apologists for the yardstick were quick to point out that it affected retail rates as well as wholesale. The wholesale price of electricity was often no more than 10 percent of the retail price; and the Alabama Power Company's wholesale rates, for example, were not far above TVA's. The real yardstick, its proponents argued, was the retail measure provided by the municipal and cooperative distributors, at rates dictated by the TVA. This theory made more sense than the wholesale yardstick notion, but it contained its own fallacies. Municipalities and cooperatives, as nonprofit public institutions, avoided the large tax burden borne by utility companies. Furthermore, the distributors of TVA power had much lower capital costs and carried a lower burden of bonded debt than did private companies. They also received valuable services from TVA, like those rendered by holding companies to their subsidiaries. TVA demanded full payment for these services, and the Authority often insisted that all charges had been properly billed. But it was hard to refute the accusation that some of the joint costs, especially promotional costs, were not fairly apportioned. One reason was that TVA's accounting system (a good one, after a wretched and embarrassing start), differed slightly from the system used by most private companies.

To achieve comparability of TVA's costs with a private company's, economists could impute interest, taxation, and all other costs not actually incurred. Within certain limits, TVA made such calculations. In early press releases on power rates Lilienthal explicitly mentioned imputed costs for making yardstick comparisons. Yet as one of TVA's highest-ranking rate experts pointed out to Lilienthal in a private memorandum, with such imputations "the 'yardstick' will be meaningless and defeated in its essential purpose."[10] Though imputed costs could hold certain factors constant for the comparison of specific variables, in the larger sense they involved circular reasoning. If the imputed figures came from private companies—the only proper source—then they could hardly contribute to a yardstick measuring the same companies' fairness and efficiency.

The truth was that the public power operations of the TVA could not provide a nationally valid economic measure of the fairness and efficiency of privately owned utilities. Though TVA produced and sold electric power alongside the C & S companies, its status as a federal agency, its multi-purpose aims, and the peculiar tax and capital position of its distributors made comparison of the two operations as unrealistic as a comparison of squares and circles. When TVA apologists, including Chairman Morgan, President Roosevelt, and especially Director Lilienthal continued to imply in public that reduced electric rates in Tupelo and other TVA-supplied cities somehow proved mismanagement or wrongdoing by utilities, the private tradition responded with justified indignation. By mid-1935 Lilienthal was complaining of the "terrific barrage on our 'yardstick' all over the country."[11]

The January 4 contract, then, failed to provide TVA and the public tradition with the showcase they had desired, at least in the strict economic sense. Though TVA never publicly admitted the deficiencies inherent in the idea, its spokesmen referred to the yardstick with steadily diminishing frequency and emphasis, especially after 1935. To public power enthusiasts, however, the chief lesson of 1934–35 in the Tennessee Valley was not that one of their pet ideas was unsound, but that Commonwealth and Southern had showed itself as perfidious as the rest of the power trust. Willkie had not upheld his end of the bargain, and TVA had not received its due under the January 4 contract. The suspicion with which Lilienthal had viewed Willkie from the beginning seemed justified, and Arthur Morgan's willingness to trust the private companies proportionally discredited. In return for limiting the area of its operations, TVA had reaped not a reward but a betrayal of the contract and a telling attack on one of its main premises.

The mutual hostility between TVA and C & S which the failure of the yardstick produced was unfortunate not only because of its effect on future relations between the two agencies but also because it tended to obscure the one solidly constructive result of TVA's power operations in the ceded territory. The rate schedule which Lilienthal had announced in 1933 was based on the hope that a cut in rates would cause a sharp rise in consumption of electricity by householders. This gamble had unquestionably paid off. The results of TVA's low rates were uniformly dramatic in the few communities where the courts allowed TVA to operate. In the Alcorn County (Mississippi) cooperative, average usage soared in three years from 49 kilowatt-hours per month to 139, as the price dropped from 5.37 cents per kilowatt-hour to 1.82. In Athens, Alabama, usage tripled while the price plummeted from 5.51 cents to 1.74 cents. In Tupelo average consumption went from 49 kilowatt-hours to 178, the price dropping from 7.40 cents to 1.58.[12]

By demonstrating that a rigorous program of rate reduction, publicity, and appliance saturation would increase consumption and thus raise the standard of living, TVA performed an exceedingly valuable service for the private tradition and for the country. It had demonstrated that elasticity of demand vastly exceeded private operators' estimates. Ontario Hydro had demonstrated it decades before, but now TVA had done it in the United States, under depression conditions and in an area noted for its poverty. The lesson was not lost on the private tradition. The "preoccupation with rates in 1935–1936," writes the historian of Detroit Edison, resulted in part from the policies of TVA and the Rural Electrification Administration, which "startled the industry as a whole into self-examination."[13]

For the private tradition the lesson was not that it should itself charge rates as low as TVA's, but that lower rates brought greatly increased consumption. It was an extraordinarily im-

portant lesson for an industry whose unit costs sharply de-
crease with increasing production. The lesson was doubly
helpful to the utilities because unlike TVA, which was backed
by the federal government, they were not financially able to
experiment radically with their rates. During the depression
the chief problem of power operators who wished to reduce
rates was that any reduction involved a temporary diminution
of revenues. Because of their heavy capital obligations, few
utilities could afford even a slight reduction of income. Should
a matured bond issue have to be defaulted, for example, the
effect on the utility's credit would be disastrous. The overcapitalization of many companies made the situation worse.
TVA's great contribution was in assuring utility men that they
could reduce rates without necessarily reducing income.

One of the first to profit from this lesson was Wendell
Willkie. Indeed he acted on the principle before the results
of the TVA experiment were in. One of the most progressive
of the utility managers, Willkie genuinely wanted to reduce
his companies' rates. Independently, but partly in anticipation
of TVA competition, his staff had devised early in 1933 an
ingenious new system which would solve the private tradition's dilemma by reducing rates without diminishing income.
Worked out even as TVA materialized, this "objective rate
plan" went into effect for the Alabama Power Company in
October 1933, two weeks after Lilienthal's announcement of
the TVA rate schedule. The Georgia company adopted it in
January and TEPCO in February 1934. By 1937 ten of Willkie's
eleven operating companies had converted to it, as had several
companies outside the C & S system. A huge success, the plan
captured the attention of the entire industry, and Willkie used
the publicity it had received in the presidential campaign
of 1940.[14]

As a writer in *Fortune* described it, the objective rate plan
was "a sort of cross between a quantity discount, a free-goods
deal, and a prize contest." It involved a dual schedule for all
domestic customers, an "immediate rate" and an "objective

rate." The immediate rate was a new schedule applied to historical data compiled for each customer, on a monthly basis for the preceding year. Had a TEPCO customer used 50 kilowatt-hours, for example, in March 1933, his "base bill" under the immediate rate would have been $2.88. If in March 1934, he used less than 50 kilowatt-hours he was billed at the immediate rate. If he used exactly 50 again, his bill was $2.88. But if he used more than 50, he was billed under the lower objective rate. For 57 kilowatt hours, his bill would have been $2.89, including six "free" kilowatt-hours. This free current was the appealing aspect of the plan, and the one most adaptable to the wide publicity accompanying the new rates. The free current for increased usage could run from one kilowatt-hour (for an increase to 19) to 438 (for an increase to 1000). With such an incentive for increased usage, the only negative aspect of the plan was that it penalized customers who already had heavy consumption, and therefore violated one of the obligations of public utilities — that they avoid discrimination within the same class of customers. But the objective rate plan was only transitional, to have effect for periods of from two to five years. At the end of the transition, when the plan had accomplished its purpose, the immediate rate became the objective rate. All customers again paid identical prices, now much lower.

The company could not lose. Its revenues would not drop unless usage dropped, a very unlikely possibility. For the C & S companies, and for many others which adopted it, the objective rate plan was an outstanding solution to a critical problem. The results in Willkie's southern companies were striking. By 1935, of all companies east of the Rockies, the top three in average customer usage were the C & S subsidiaries in Georgia, Alabama, and Tennessee. TEPCO led all companies in gain over 1934. Its rates dropped accordingly, from 5.77 cents per kilowatt-hour in 1933, when the national average was 5.49, to 3.63 cents in 1935, when the national average was 5.03.[15]

The undertaking by Willkie's companies of the objective rate plan bore out the contention of public power advocates that limited public ownership could accomplish "regulation by example" which would prove more effective than regulation by commissions. Norris and others had long observed that in areas surrounding public power plants, such as those in Los Angeles and Seattle, private companies' rates were unusually low. The apparent meaning of this phenomenon was that where potential competition existed the public plant served as a powerful incentive for the adjacent private company to lower its rates. Failure to do so invited a public ownership movement in its own territory. This was not competition in the usual sense, but competition by halo effect, or by example. It was the hope of such men as Lilienthal, Morris L. Cooke, and Leland Olds that TVA would perform such a function on a large scale. C & S's inauguration of the objective rate plan suggested that TVA had done just that, despite Willkie's dubious claim that it was all a coincidence.

The months following the signing of the January 4 contract were in many ways as unsatisfactory to Commonwealth and Southern as to the TVA. Willkie's task, as president of a major holding company, was not only to prevent injury to his operating companies in the Tennessee Valley, but also to defend privately-owned utilities against all other attacks from the public tradition. The TVA was the first front in the Roosevelt administration's power program, but it was not the only one. The president's well-known antipathy to holding companies, his determination to bring electricity to farmers, and his powerful conviction that rates everywhere should be much lower served notice that the private tradition could expect from the New Deal a diversified and prolonged attack.

In anticipation of such an attack, Willkie had instituted a number of internal reforms of both the Commonwealth and Southern holding company structure and of some of its operating companies. From its inception C & S had been a well-run organization, and there was not nearly so much to reform here as there was in most holding companies. "I am frank to say to you," Senator Burton K. Wheeler told Willkie during hearings on holding company legislation in 1935, "that probably if there had not been any more abuses in some companies than there have been in yours ... you probably would not have been faced with some of the provisions you are faced with." Shortly after his elevation to C & S's presidency Willkie had simplified its corporate structure, replaced the bankers on its board with such operating company executives as Preston Arkwright and Josephus Conn Guild, refinanced aggressively to take advantage of depression-cheap money, begun an enormous appliance sales program to build load and increase usage (partly in cooperation with TVA, as Lilienthal had hoped), and inaugurated the highly successful objective rate plan.[16]

Of the three major C & S subsidiaries in the southern group, the Alabama and Georgia companies enjoyed high esteem within the industry. The third, TEPCO, the one most directly threatened by TVA, suffered from several unfortunate aspects of its history. It had grown up around Chattanooga, and later Nashville, in a series of mergers of fiercely competitive companies formerly devoted to running each other out of business. One result was a sizable overcapitalization, and TEPCO lacked the financial strength of its sister companies to withstand the impact of the depression. Although it operated a dam on the Tennessee River, TEPCO had the lowest power generating capacity of the three companies. It also charged the highest rates, and had the least average consumption by its domestic customers. It therefore benefited most from the reforms instituted by Willkie.[17] The rub was that none of these reforms made the company's territory any less attractive to TVA's power planners. Indeed, the more TEPCO developed its markets, the more inviting those markets became.

In June 1933, the month of TVA's incorporation, the Tennessee utilities commission ordered the company to simplify and reduce its rates. TEPCO anticipated a consequent drop in revenue of about 10 percent. In its unfavorable financial position, the company now faced a very dangerous situation, compounded by the TVA threat. The only solution, president Guild and other managers decided, was to launch an all-out campaign to build a greater volume of business.[18]

Besides doubling its sales force, TEPCO enlisted two-thirds of its 3,000 employees as part-time salesmen, styling the operation a "world cruise" aboard the *S.S. President Guild*. The crew, comprising linemen, clerks, bus drivers, and meter readers, energetically set about saturating the company's territory with refrigerators, ranges, irons, and water heaters. Though the campaign at times became almost ludicrous (besides the world cruise there was a "rocket trip to the planets"), it paid handsome rewards. With promotions overlapping each other in periods such as "Willkie Month," the company by 1937 had doubled its appliance load. In 1934 it received the Edison Electric Institute's annual Coffin Award, for having achieved "one of the most, if not the most, remarkable sales increases in residential, commercial, and industrial power in the history of the Electrical Industry." In the next year TEPCO led every other company in the United States in growth of average customer usage, through its combination of appliance saturation with the objective rate plan.[19]

Although internal reforms both benefited the C & S companies and brought their operations more closely into line with the standards proposed by their critics, they afforded Willkie and his industry no real security from political attacks. In the early months of the New Deal, urgent affairs of relief and recovery monopolized Roosevelt's time, but by the fall of 1934 there were signs that the utilities might soon expect a siege in earnest. First, long investigations by the Federal Trade Commission and the House Interstate Commerce Committee pointed toward a holding company bill. Second, PWA's grants and loans for public electric systems in cities scattered

throughout the country suggested serious government competition. Third, Roosevelt was about to create a Rural Electrification Administration. And fourth, from various sources
came such legislation as amendments to the TVA Act, a Federal Power Act, and a bill instructing the Federal Power
Commission to ascertain and publish comparative rate schedules for the nation.

Though all these administration plans were inimical to
private power interests, they evolved piecemeal and not as
parts of a coordinated policy. The lack of an announced, well
defined policy made the New Deal's attack even more disturbing to the public utility industry than it might have been.
Morris L. Cooke, a leading public power spokesman, realized
the disadvantages which the absence of a stated government
policy posed for the industry as well as for the administration,
and urged the creation of a body which could formulate and
enunciate a comprehensive policy statement. "Electric power
is as basic to the New Deal as soil conservation, land use, or
credit," Cooke wrote to Harold Ickes, "and in many highly
significant moves of the Administration is so recognized. Yet
there is no adequate national power policy coordinating isolated new moves and without this it is small wonder that some
of these moves seem opportunistic if not illogical and give rise
to unwarranted criticism." In making this observation Cooke
identified one of the most persistent and serious problems of
New Deal power policy. It was a problem that plagued the
TVA and the fourteen other agencies and departments concerned with power, and even more plagued the private electric industry, which had great difficulty learning just what the
New Deal's attitude was. Speculation within the industry
ranged from fearful predictions that Roosevelt would ultimately try to nationalize all electric utilities to more accurate
guesses that he merely wished thorough reform. Like other
businessmen in the 1930s, utility executives seldom knew
precisely where they stood. For their own peace of mind, and
for the planning of their business operations, they wished

above all to know the fullest details of the government's policy. As Cooke noted,

> If such a uniform and all-inclusive policy is not decided upon fairly immediately there is every reason to expect, not only that there will be the equivalent of competition between public plants, but also that the acerbities in the competition between public and private plants will be unnecessarily aggravated and that uneconomical strife even within the industry may result.

Following Cooke's suggestion, Ickes in 1934 persuaded Roosevelt to appoint a National Power Policy Committee. The original members were Ickes (Chairman); Cooke (Vice-chairman); Robert M. Healy of the Securities and Exchange Commission, who had directed the FTC's long investigation of the utility industry; Lilienthal of the TVA; Frank McNinch of the Federal Power Commission; Elwood Mead, Commissioner of Reclamation; and T. W. Norcross, chief engineer of the Forest Service. The NPPC set up offices inside the Public Works Administration, which funded it with a grant of $100,000.[20]

The need for coordination was real, but the National Power Policy Committee proved inadequate to the task. In the first eighteen months of its existence the committee held only four meetings, and each was an exercise in indecision and interdepartmental jealousy. At the first meeting, for example, Lilienthal tried to enlist the committee's help in TVA's legal problems and its troubles with the Alabama utilities commission, which claimed jurisdiction over it. Reluctant to do anything important for fear of taking a false step or offending Roosevelt, the committee refused Lilienthal's request. At another meeting Chairman McNinch of the Federal Power Commission seemed to think the committee was invading the sphere of the FPC, and said that the president's policy was already clear from his Portland speech. Actually the committee's lackadaisical performance derived largely from its members' overriding loyalty to their own agencies and from a general failure to see the power question as a whole. Repeatedly men such as Cooke and the NPPC'S executive secretary, Joel David Wolfsohn, pleaded with the group to enunciate a broad policy, but to no avail. The committee lapsed into virtual inactivity, to be twice resurrected, in 1937 and 1939, when urgent problems arose.[21]

The NPPC did have one outstanding product. The committee's early meetings found all members in agreement that something must be done about holding companies. For this task the committee borrowed from PWA Benjamin V. Cohen, who became the NPPC's general counsel. Cohen, a brilliant disciple of Felix Frankfurter, immediately went to work drafting comprehensive legislation for federal regulation of holding companies. Typically, Roosevelt had put other agencies to work on the same problem, and Cohen had trouble coordinating the government's various positions. He received little help from the holding company executives he consulted; except for Willkie, not one was ready to accept anything more than superficial federal regulation. After long conferences with the staffs of various agencies and with the president, Cohen finally completed his draft bill. On February 6, 1935, Burton K. Wheeler introduced it in the Senate, and Sam Rayburn in the House.[22]

The Wheeler-Rayburn bill ignited one of the most intensive and scandalous lobbying campaigns in American history, a campaign that in itself seemed to validate the conclusions of the long FTC investigation which preceded the bill. The specific target of the power interests was the "death sentence" clause, which authorized the Securities and Exchange Commission to dissolve within five years any utility holding company that could not prove its usefulness. Roosevelt had made the death sentence an explicit test of a Congressman's loyalty to the New Deal.

The fight was the most bitter that Washington observers had seen in years, and it represented the first effective challenge to the New Deal's congressional juggernaut. Lobbyists poured into the capital. An avalanche of mail and telegrams, some of them phony, buried the desks of legislators. Even the Congressman from the Muscle Shoals district, Lilienthal wrote Frankfurter, "has been terrified, reporting in an injured tone that he has received six thousand letters from his constituents objecting to his 'anti-utility' votes. That is in a district in which we [TVA] have four thousand men employed and have aided in the economic condition in the lives of 50,000 people."[23] Ultimately the situation became so bad that both houses of Congress investigated the lobbying, and their findings probably saved the more stringent of the bill's many provisions from defeat.

Wendell Willkie, for the first time rising to national prominence as a passionate defender of private enterprise, stood out as the most conspicuous of the utility spokesmen. He led the stream of executives who testified against the bill before Senate and House Committees, wrote articles for national magazines, and made several well-publicized speeches. The holding company bill, he told a CBS radio audience, "is revolutionary in nature, drastic in provision, will be destructive in operation and, if passed, will have great deflationary influence and serve as a further hurdle for business recovery." Predicting that the bill's passage would send the entire industry "into a chaos of liquidation and receiverships," Willkie appealed in ominous tones to the fears of other businessmen. "Do you for a moment believe," he asked conventioneers of the national Chamber of Commerce, "that if the principle of the right of Congress to dissolve [corporations] by legislative fiat... is applied to us, that the rest of you for long will remain free from its application?" Later Willkie would claim authorship of the phrase "death sentence" which helped stiffen opposition to the bill.[24]

The fight persisted into the spring and summer of 1935, turbulent months that witnessed the Supreme Court's invali-

dation of the National Industrial Recovery Act and the Farm
Mortgage Moratorium law; and, with the Emergency Relief
Appropriation of $4.8 billion, the beginning of the largest
welfare program in American history.

By vote of 45–44, the Senate approved the death sentence
in mid-June. But three weeks later, the House rejected it,
216–146, and Congress was deadlocked. In the end Roosevelt
had to compromise and settle for a milder version of the death
sentence. He still won his main objectives. It was a very
stringent bill that he signed on August 26, and it represented
a victory over one of the richest war chests ever collected to
fight a single piece of legislation. The Wheeler-Rayburn Act
authorized the SEC to dissolve holding companies more than
twice removed from their operating companies, and those
whose systems were incapable of physical interconnection or
integration. All holding companies must register with the
SEC, which wielded broad powers over their financial dealings. "As far as I am personally concerned in my duty as
trustee to 200,000 utility security holders," said Willkie, "I
have only one possible regret, if by spending more money
legitimately the Commonwealth & Southern could have prevented this destructive Act from being passed, that I did not
authorize such additional expenditure."[25]

For the New Deal the holding company act was a smashing
victory, but a costly one. On several key votes in both houses,
the Democratic party had split. The fissure was one of the
earliest signs of the emergence of a conservative congressional coalition which later in the decade would stifle some of
Roosevelt's major legislation.[26]

The holding company brouhaha had nothing to do directly
with TVA, but it had three important side effects. The first
was an unlucky complication of issues in TVA's request of
1935 for amendments to the Act of 1933. The second appeared
later, when TVA acquired small, isolated pieces of holding
company properties lopped off by SEC action. The third was
the conspicuous new status of Wendell Willkie as the most

formidable anti-New Deal spokesman in the entire business community. Willkie's new prominence tended to invest his battle with TVA with much broader national importance.

Only slightly less disturbing to the private tradition than the holding company act was the activity of the Public Works Administration. PWA, as an unemployment relief agency, had authority to provide funds for the construction (but not purchase) of municipal electric systems. It had come into being in June 1933 under Title II of the National Industrial Recovery Act. With an appropriation of $3.3 billion, it was the New Deal's chief recovery program in the field of public works, a field the Hoover administration had already begun to cultivate. Under the cautious control of the egotistical and irascible Harold L. Ickes, PWA spent too slowly to help recovery in any spectacular way. But Ickes, if he did not spend too well, spent wisely. PWA money eventually funded the Bonneville, Grand Coulee, and Fort Peck dams, and built such landmarks as New York's Triborough Bridge and Lincoln Tunnel, such famous ships as the aircraft carriers *Enterprise* and *Yorktown*.[27]

Administrator Ickes, who for many years was a thorn in the flesh of Chicago's Samuel Insull, felt that PWA, like TVA, should perform auxiliary regulation of the utilities as well as stimulate economic recovery. He sometimes used the threat of a competing public system to beat down the rates of private companies, and he once declared that even if the proposed PWA-funded plants charged rates higher than those of the existing private systems he might still authorize their construction. "It has been my position," he stated boldly, "that there are definite intangible values flowing to a community that owns and operates its own utilities." By the middle of 1935 PWA had received 495 applications for public power projects, had secured rate reductions in some that it rejected, and had made 145 allotments totalling almost $50 million. Beginning in 1935, 45 percent of individual allotments could be outright gifts to the municipalities, the remainder being low-interest loans.[28]

To the TVA the PWA program was of vital, almost definitive importance, and the two agencies worked together so closely that Willkie and his lawyers formally charged conspiracy. By 1936 PWA had allotted a total of $10 million to nine cities in Alabama, two in Mississippi, and eight in Tennessee for the construction of municipal plants that would hook up to TVA's power lines. The utilities contested almost all of these allotments in court.[29] The delay caused by this litigation, together with a fusillade of other lawsuits against PWA all over the country and against TVA in federal and state courts, greatly retarded the power programs of both agencies. Not until 1938 and 1939 did the Supreme Court validate both programs. In the meantime the litigation not only delayed the expenditure of relief money but also deepened the mutual bitterness between the public and private traditions.

Roosevelt prescribed still more unpleasant medicine for the private companies when he created the Rural Electrification Administration.[30] Power lines served only 10 percent of the nation's farms in 1933, and rural electrification had long been one of Roosevelt's pet projects. Instituted by executive order during the holding company legislative fight in 1935, the Rural Electrification Administration became permanent a year later through the Norris-Rayburn Act. REA operated chiefly as a lending agency, channeling funds both to private companies and to rural cooperatives. The original ten-year plan authorized the Reconstruction Finance Corporation to provide REA with $50 million for its first year, with congressional appropriations of up to $40 million for each of the next nine years. But appropriations soon grew much larger.

The history of REA in several ways paralleled that of TVA. Early attempts at cooperation with privately owned utilities failed, despite the patient efforts of the first administrator, the aristocratic and ubiquitous Morris L. Cooke. Cooke wanted to use private as well as public agencies in order to accelerate the progress of REA, but the companies refused to cooperate. After about six months' debate within the industry, the private power men decided not to accept REA money, and only 3.5 percent of the first year's loans went to private companies. They could secure private loans with interest rates almost as low as those REA offered, and without the controls over policy that REA exercised. Instead, the private tradition embarked energetically on its own overdue program in rural electrification. Naturally the REA claimed credit for this newfound vigor. The important point is that both private and public agencies did excellent work. By 1950 almost 80 percent of the nation's farms had electricity, compared with only about 11 percent in 1935. Few New Deal programs achieved such striking gains.

The success came in a heated atmosphere. Like TVA, REA had serious problems both with the private tradition and within the agency itself, though its internal troubles were not as severe as TVA's. Senator Norris, the sponsor of legislation for both agencies, wished neither one to cooperate or compromise with the power trust. He opposed Administrator Cooke's policy of offering loans to private companies. Cooke changed his policy, but this conflict and others involving REA were distasteful to him. Pleading poor health, he resigned in 1937. John Carmody, his replacement and a true believer in the cooperative movement, vigorously promoted rural co-ops and made rapid progress.

As the situation between the public and private traditions became increasingly polarized, so did the relationship between Arthur Morgan and David Lilienthal. The failure of Commonwealth and Southern to honor the January 4 contract increased the directors' animosity toward each other. When Morgan continued to espouse a policy of cooperation with Willkie's companies, despite their tactics of delay, propaganda, and litigation, relations between him and Lilienthal steadily deteriorated. The Chairman came to regard Lilienthal

as a devious political operator who was not in the least reluctant to try to beat the private tradition at its own games of
legal maneuver, obstructionism, and misleading publicity.
Viewing the TVA as a social experiment of crucial national
importance, Morgan feared that Lilienthal's tactics would
ruin the Authority's integrity. With some justification, Morgan
felt that his colleague was attempting to undermine him and
seize control of the organization for the narrow purpose of
furthering Lilienthal's personal career.[31]

Lilienthal regarded Morgan as a talented but naive and
visionary utopian who posed a double threat to the power
program. First, Morgan's loose talk and writing about TVA's
social missions created skepticism among the public and
among tough-minded congressmen whose continued good
will TVA needed. To Lilienthal, Morgan seemed to lack the
most elementary appreciation of the need to keep the Authority's political fences mended. Second, Morgan's apparent
naivete concerning the nature of TVA's opposition in the
power fight represented for Lilienthal a constant peril.
Morgan, who believed in the kind of cooperation between
government and business embodied in the National Recovery Administration, shared none of Lilienthal's fear and wariness of utility executives. A thorough believer in the gospel
of efficiency that had motivated the conservation program of
Theodore Roosevelt, Morgan went out of his way to avoid
squabbles with the private tradition. Rather than using TVA
as an instrument for effecting the triumph of the people over
the interests, Morgan wished to show what magnificent social
benefits could flow from a rational, planned economic development of the Tennessee basin.[32]

By the fall of 1935 Morgan had concluded that Lilienthal
must be replaced. Of the directors' staggered terms of office,
Lilienthal had drawn the shortest of the original three, and
his appointment would expire in May 1936. Morgan discussed
the situation with Roosevelt at a meeting in Warm Springs.
The president, who probably did not fully apprehend the

seriousness of the problem, tentatively agreed with Morgan. When, in a typical turnabout, Roosevelt began to waver, Morgan lobbied in Washington, taking his case to men such as Norris and Ickes, both of whom he told that he himself would resign if Lilienthal were reappointed. Intrigue on both sides then plunged the TVA staff into a confusion of uncertainty and divided loyalties. Roosevelt reappointed Lilienthal over Morgan's objection, and essentially did nothing further to resolve the feud. From that point until Morgan's forced departure from the TVA two years later (he reneged on his threat to resign), the situation within the board of directors was one of extreme delicacy and ill will. Its effect on the fight between TVA and Commonwealth and Southern was to complicate an already tangled problem.

The private tradition, convinced that it was fighting for its existence, responded to the administration's actions of 1934–1935 with direct attacks in the courts. "It is with regret," wrote Willkie in his report to C & S stockholders for 1935, "that your officers find it necessary to report to you concerning so much litigation." Undertaken "with extreme reluctance," it was the only policy available "to preserve your and the Corporation's property from ruthless destruction."[33]

At first the power companies did not participate directly in the TVA litigation. The Ashwander case was begun by fourteen preferred stockholders of the Alabama Power Company, not by the company itself. The suit started at a time when it appeared that TVA at last was making headway in persuading Willkie to fulfill the terms of the January 4 contract. On February 26, 1935, just when it seemed that the Chemical Bank might compromise on its refusal to release the sale property, a federal judge decreed in the Ashwander case that TVA be enjoined from completing parts of the January 4 contract. The peculiar chronology of these events — the refusal of the companies to accept municipal bonds in payment for the distribution systems, the exasperating behavior of the Chemical Bank, and now the injunction — suggested to Lilienthal and others in the TVA that Willkie's strategy had been to delay the transaction until the courts could be summoned to the private tradition's rescue. For his part Willkie heatedly denied any connection with the Ashwander case, despite circumstantial evidence tying him to its prosecution.[34] In the meantime, a similar suit enjoining TVA's purchase of the Knoxville utility and a barrage of litigation against PWA also delayed TVA's acquisition of a large yardstick market.

To the private tradition the New Deal's manifold activities in the power field — TVA, REA, PWA, the Public Utility Holding Company Act — seemed a concerted and prejudiced attack by their own government. With increasing paranoia the private utility men responded in kind. Litigation became increasingly serious. Propaganda grew more and more vicious. By 1936 relations between the government and the power industry were thoroughly polarized, and the atmosphere was one of mutual hatred. The hope of cooperation and amicable relations which had seemed to exist in January 1934 was now quite dead. When Roosevelt began in the fall of 1936 an important attempt at broad settlement, the situation was not in the least conducive to its success.

5

THE POWER POOL

ROOSEVELT'S PROGRAM HAD helped to create some perplexing economic problems. A potential oversupply of power and competitive scramble for markets threatened the Tennessee Valley and the Pacific Northwest, as federal hydro dams in those areas neared completion. Utility companies facing public competition found their standing in the investment market impaired, and were unable to take advantage of depression-cheap money by refunding their bonds. The industry as a whole was delaying new construction, and thus undermining national recovery, until Roosevelt changed or clarified his policy, or until the courts struck down his program.

Of the variety of remedies suggested for these problems, the most ingenious was a plan called the "power pool." Introduced early in 1936, it became the focus of the power question in the fall of that year, only to be summarily abandoned in January 1937. A road considered but not taken, the power pool revealed the differing aims within the Roosevelt administration as clearly as did any policy actually instituted.

The idea originated with Alexander Sachs, who after serving as an economic planner with the National Recovery Administration had returned as director of research to the Lehman Corporation, and investment firm interested in utility finance. Sachs, a Democrat and friend of Hugh Johnson, was a colorful character whose flamboyant prose (in support of his proposal he adduced Plato and Herodotus, among others) disguised a hard precision of thought about the American economy.

According to Sachs's plan, public and private producers of electricity would pool resources for their own and the consumers' benefit, instead of competing with each other and causing economic waste. As the federal hydro projects in the West and Southeast went forward, great blocks of electricity were about to become available in areas with insufficient demand, setting the stage for an intense competition for markets. This competition would help neither federal nor private agencies, and would burden the public regardless of who won. Sachs believed that a cooperative pooling and coordination of production, perhaps eventually on a national scale, would provide a much sounder economic arrangement and a variety of social benefits.[1]

Since the area of immediate danger was the Tennessee Valley, the plan would first be tried there. Suppliers of electricity, chiefly TVA and Commonwealth and Southern, would sell their power not to consumers but to a newly-created pool organization. This agency, staffed with government and utility representatives, would then distribute electricity to municipal, cooperative, and private retailers at a uniform and predetermined wholesale price. Power resources would thus be integrated into a system similar to the British Grid, in which public and private agencies coordinated their operations for mutual economies. All Valley customers, not only those who bought TVA electricity, would benefit from the federal program. The cost of transmitted power would drop by 15 to 25 percent. Private companies could draw on TVA's production and temporarily avoid having to build expensive new generating plants to meet the growth of consumption under the objective rate plan. The pool would settle the TVA-C & S fight and permit the companies to refinance their bonded debts. One estimate was that this refunding, already accomplished in Willkie's northern group, would save his southern companies about $6 million annually, and permit another big cut in rates.[2]

The pool would solve one of TVA's biggest problems too, by absorbing the power from its new dams. Furthermore, it would demonstrate that the Authority cared more about serving consumers than about punishing utility companies. If properly designed the pool would provide an alternative to the yardstick, yet still show the effect of low rates on consumer demand. According to the plan the pool agency was to purchase the cheapest power first, irrespective of who produced it. TVA therefore could demonstrate its self-proclaimed superiority. Tupelo and other cities would continue their retail yardstick operations by charging low rates and challenging the private distributors to match them. Part of the political agitation would remain, but most of it would not directly involve TVA. And the broad negotiations might provide an opening to bargain for a larger public power area. The Authority still wanted to convert the TEPCO region to public power, and to do so TVA planners were thinking more and more of a straight purchase of the company. Such a purchase would not necessarily conflict with the Sachs plan, since the pool applied mainly to transmission. TVA wanted to increase public distribution, by promoting the shift of Tennessee communities away from TEPCO toward municipal public power. TVA envisioned a joint purchase of the company, with the Authority buying the generation and transmission facilities and the cities the distribution. If the pool materialized, the transmission lines would come under the jurisdiction of the pool, but the distribution systems would still be public power yardsticks.[3]

President Roosevelt was captivated by the pooling idea, though he failed to appreciate its complexity or the division of opinion about it within his administration. Prosposals for implementing the pool ranged from a simple contractual agreement whereby TVA and C & S would interchange only

the power surplus to their own immediate needs, to an elaborate reordering of the whole utility question through a corporation created by Congress to administer a grid. However
implemented, the plan raised difficult questions. What should
be the relative strength of public and private representation
on the pool agency? What valuation methods should be used
to determine the cheapest power source? Should PWA allotments continue in the Tennessee Valley? Should the pool
affect retail rates directly, or only indirectly by reducing
wholesale rates? Should the companies continue to challenge
TVA and PWA in court? Should there be a division of territory, or should TVA continue to solicit Willkie's customers?[4]

Despite these unanswered questions, the potential gains
to the public, the TVA, and the private companies made the
proposal an eminently sensible solution to some of the problems raised by the New Deal's power program. "The present
status," as Willkie wrote Roosevelt, "is practically one of
open warfare and, as long as that status continues, the utilities in that [Tennessee Valley] district naturally feel that they
are fighting for their lives and are obliged to defend themselves by every legitimate means,"—means which included
a number of lawsuits against the government, "the necessity for which," wrote Willkie, "no one regrets more than
I do."[5]

For Lilienthal, who had mentioned the benefits of a power
pool to his colleagues as early as February 1936, some sort
of settlement was economically desirable, but the question
was also political. The kind of "broad-scale, long-time, so-
called permanent adjustment" advocated by Arthur Morgan
was a nice ideal, wrote Lilienthal. But on both sides the power
question was "still too heated to permit the successful negotiation of such an arrangement." Instead, the power director
wanted TVA to protect itself by working toward its own independent operating system, with yardstick "spots" and
large industrial customers. The ultimate objective could re-
semble a power pool, but for the moment TVA had enough
problems.[6]

Lilienthal greatly feared that the grid plan would shift the initiative and control of the situation away from TVA, and divert the public's attention from the Authority at a critical time. "I will tell you frankly," he said to Sachs, "we are [a] good deal disturbed about any division of responsibility." If the president wished to assign the problem to Sachs or to another agency such as the Federal Power Commission, "I think he ought to tell us so." The problem was already quite complicated, and the addition of new participants like Sachs could hardly help matters. To others Lilienthal complained of the "unnecessarily grandiose stuff on a comprehensive solution" being offered Roosevelt by proponents of the power pool.[7]

At first, Willkie also belittled the plan, for the same old reason that it afforded his companies no "certainty" against continued raiding by TVA and PWA. Unless the new arrangement provided such certainty, his companies could not refinance, and one of the principal virtues of the power pool, as envisioned by Sachs, would never materialize. Willkie had now come to the point of willingness to sell the entire Tennessee Electric Power Company if TVA would only stay out of the rest of C & S's market area. Once the old TEPCO area came under public power, TVA would have no electricity available to sell outside the territory. The situation would parallel that contemplated by the January 4 contract, but TVA would at last have a large, integrated yardstick area.[8]

Lilienthal stuck to his refusal to promise any such thing, on the grounds that it would violate the preference clause in the TVA Act. The Authority began a staff study of the power pool and its variations, but not with the idea that pooling would restrict the growth of public power in the Tennessee Valley.

In the meantime, the ripening Morgan-Lilienthal feud had erupted into open war over this very question of territorial restriction, now an urgent problem because the January 4 contract would soon expire. Supported by Harcourt

Morgan, Lilienthal in August 1936 pushed through a 2–1 board resolution prohibiting any future agreement by TVA to stay out of Willkie's territory. Outvoted, Chairman Arthur Morgan insisted on appealing the decision to Roosevelt.[9]

With the presidential election staring him in the face, Roosevelt wanted above all to avoid doing anything controversial. Though by now he agreed in principle with Lilienthal, "It is absolutely impossible for me," he wrote the board, "between now and [the election], to go into the policy problem." Instead, Roosevelt suggested putting off the immediate issue by simply extending the life of the January 4 contract.[10] The extension could be the first item on the agenda of a broad conference he had planned for a discussion of the power pool. The "truce" symbolized by the extension would start the pooling negotiations off on the right foot. With a single gesture, Roosevelt could thus accomplish several different things—sidetrack the problem of territorial boundaries, enhance the prospects for a successful power pool, and take a small step toward ultimate peace with the utilities, a step which might win him some votes without losing him others. As events would show, these aims not only clashed with each other, they clashed with the aims of Roosevelt's subordinates, particularly Lilienthal, who had his own notions of what the power pool discussions might accomplish.

The president went ahead with his plans, however, sending personal invitations to a conference based on "the cooperation of the Tennessee Valley Authority and the private utility companies in that region."[11] Roosevelt invited Alexander Sachs, the originator of the idea; Louis Wehle, a nephew of Justice Brandeis and an expert on the law of public corporations; the TVA board of directors; Frederic Delano, chairman of the National Resources Committee; Morris L. Cooke of the Rural Electrification Administration; Chairman Frank McNinch and Vice-Chairman Basil Manly of the Federal Power Commission; Samuel Ferguson, a forward-looking utility manager whose Hartford Electric Light Company had pioneered the technical aspects of power pooling; Wendell Willkie of the Commonwealth and Southern Corporation; Preston Arkwright of the Georgia Power Company; Owen D. Young of General Electric; and Russell Leffingwell of Morgan and Company.

The high distinction of this group suggested that Roosevelt meant to transact serious business. Yet reporters and commentators speculated that this well-publicized conference, called just seven weeks before the presidential election, was in fact a political ploy. By adopting a conciliatory attitude toward utilities, Roosevelt could appear to be accommodating business in general, and he might pick up votes previously conceded to Landon. The mere invitation to the conference was the apparent cause of a 15 percent rise in the trading price of C & S stock.[12]

Yet Roosevelt showed every indication of sincerity. His overall strategy in this campaign was avowedly anti-"economic royalist"—the reverse of conciliation. He loved dramatic gestures of this kind, and the power pool obviously appealed to him. "One thing is quite clear to me," Louis Wehle wrote, "namely, that the President is wholly serious about this matter; that he views a pooling arrangement as a highly important objective, and that he fully intends to pursue it for the purpose of stabilizing conditions on a fair basis." Roosevelt could now afford to make a generous gesture. The Holding Company and Federal Power Acts of 1935 had the utilities on the defensive, and the favorable Supreme Court decision of February 1936 in the Ashwander case had raised TVA's prestige. Willkie, furthermore, was anxious to get an extension of the January 4 contract, and could be expected to be more cooperative than usual.[13]

Nevertheless, the president did not appreciate the extent of division within his own ranks. The militant public power spokesmen in Congress—Norris, La Follette, and Rankin—recoiled at the notion of pooling interests with TVA's enemies, and registered their objections in strong language. The informal advisers Sachs and Wehle had much bigger expectations for the scope and success of the plan than did the government conferees. The Federal Power Commission's chairman totally opposed the pool, but his vice-chairman enthusiastically supported it. And inside the TVA Morgan and Lilienthal were again hopelessly split.

For Lilienthal, the pool was indeed a ploy, not so much to win votes for Roosevelt, but to show up the utilities as antisocial institutions. In Lilienthal's opinion the idea had little chance of practical success but great potential for propaganda. "The companies won't accept this proposal now, of course," he wrote Senator La Follette, "but it seemed to me important to put them on record on this really sensible proposal." To Norris Lilienthal wrote that the power pool would "constitute a complete answer to any criticism against the alleged waste involved in TVA building more transmission lines than the area, considered as a unit, actually required." Despite the likelihood of a rejection, he told Norris, "it does seem to me wise to put forward such a plan, at least in broad outline, so that the public is constantly aware that there is no lack of a desire to do the reasonable thing so far as the TVA is concerned, as long as the plan puts the public interest first." Lilienthal's only fear was that TVA might lose its initiative. "I am greatly concerned," he wrote Frankfurter, that the utilities "are going to take the ball away from the President on this issue," unless Roosevelt clearly defined the scope of the negotiations so as to preserve the gains already made in the power fight.[14] Though he gave Roosevelt a firm endorsement of the plan, Lilienthal was in no mood to make important concessions, regardless of what TVA and the public might receive in return. His main objective for the power pool was to demonstrate the hypocrisy of the private tradition by showing that it was more interested in profit-making than in service.

Arthur Morgan, on the other hand, viewed pooling as a unique opportunity to settle the whole power question fairly—

to establish a reasonable national policy, to broaden the benefits of the federal program, to deal honorably with Willkie and his stockholders, and to eliminate the policy basis of his own dispute with Lilienthal. Accordingly, Morgan did not intend to take a passive role in the conference, and as he said later, "I considered it my duty to be prepared."[15]

His method of preparation sent Lilienthal into a near panic and got the negotiations off to a wretched start. Assisted by George W. Hamilton, the former chief engineer of Insull's Middle West Utilities system, Morgan prepared a twenty-two page memorandum on the proposed pool and showed it to private conferees before Roosevelt's scheduled meeting even began. Hastily drafted, the paper served no useful purpose. As a TVA consultant pointed out, "Dr. Morgan, throughout the memorandum, has well stated the position of the Commonwealth and Southern Corporation." The chairman's unfamiliarity with the vocabulary of utility regulation caused him to "take at face value the fine phraseology which has been coined." Outraged, Lilienthal wrote Norris that the memorandum presented "the views of the Chairman of one of the negotiating parties, in advance of the negotiations – views which are made available in advance to the other side." Even worse, Morgan had listed a number of "rights of private interests the public representative is ready not only to concede, but to urge." Finally, Morgan had written his memorandum with the assistance of an engineer who "had been closely identified for some twenty years with Samuel and Martin Insull."[16]

Actually the mere assistance of Hamilton did not prove treachery by Morgan. Most engineers who knew anything about power had learned it by working for private companies. But the text of Morgan's memorandum was itself disturbing. Norris, immediately after receiving Lilienthal's report, wrote President Roosevelt that he was "dumbfounded" by the memorandum and convinced, "against my will," that Morgan had "gone over to the enemy."[17]

The attitude of the key government representative, Lilienthal, thus began to shift fatefully from wary approval of the power pool as a tactical thrust to strong disapproval of it for any purpose. The blunder of the Morgan memorandum and the multiple splits in the lines of the public power representatives were bad enough. But now Lilienthal worried deeply about the ambiguous roles of Alexander Sachs and Louis Wehle, both of whom seemed to have gained Roosevelt's ear. Both were supposed to be neutral, but both were new to the power fight and seemed insufficiently aware of the need to preserve gains already made by the New Deal.

Roosevelt, only dimly aware of these difficulties, which he himself had aggravated by telling different conferees different things, went ahead with his plans. At Lilienthal's suggestion the government representatives met privately among themselves before the main conference, and this early meeting revealed again the policy split within the government. Roosevelt therefore decided to restrict the White House conference to matters about which substantial agreement already existed.[18]

At the main conference, on September 30, 1936, the six public, five private, and two neutral members strung themselves out in a single row of chairs, all facing Roosevelt. "There was no fraternization," recalled Louis Wehle, "no preliminary pipe of peace. Weapons did not seem to have been left outside." Roosevelt began amiably, referring to the cooperation of private and public power interests in Europe and to his own successful mediation of a dispute between South American republics. He said the TVA-C & S impasse could be resolved in the same way. A discussion of the power pool then began, but degenerated quickly into an argument between Lilienthal and Willkie over the fairness of the yardstick and TVA's "stealing" of Willkie's customers. Roosevelt recommended that the agencies directly concerned with pooling—TVA, C & S, and the Federal Power Commission—continue the engineering studies necessary to a broad agreement. The studies would take several weeks and get Roosevelt through the election period without his having to make any commitment.[19]

For the immediate problem of the expiration of the January 4 contract, Lilienthal proposed a thirty-day continuance with no mention of territorial restrictions. Willkie, affecting surprise and injury, suggested six months with the same provisions as to territory already provided in the existing contract. After some discussion Roosevelt directed Louis Wehle to act as a "professor of English" in bringing the parties to agreement on the details and duration of the extension. Thus Wehle, a private citizen who had not even wished to come to the conference, now received the formidable assignment of mediating between Lilienthal and Willkie. His task was made doubly hard by Roosevelt's failure to make clear his policy, during the upcoming "truce" period, with respect to PWA grants and TVA inroads in C & S territory.[20]

After a week of exhausting negotiations, held together mainly by Wehle's determination, TVA and C & S signed a three-month extension of the January 4 contract. The announcement of the signing suggested a happy augur of peace between the public and private traditions. Actually the truce was illusory. The parties were unable to agree whether the extension, which they had just signed, barred the Authority from all of Willkie's territory for three months (Willkie's view), from only that part of it not ceded by the January 4 contract (Lilienthal's view), or from none of it.[21]

Except for Chattanooga, the home of TEPCO and the main trouble spot in the contest between Lilienthal and Willkie, the truce agreement did not apply to territory at all. And only Roosevelt's specific request had forced Lilienthal to stay out of Chattanooga. After a referendum in favor of public power, officials of that city had negotiated with TVA for several months, and had finally signed a contract to purchase TVA power. Only the January 4 contract, which barred the Author-

ity from Chattanooga, had prevented TVA from signing the
agreement too, and thereby taking the first step toward driv-
ing TEPCO out of business. When Willkie complained of
this threat during the White House conference, Roosevelt
asked that TVA withhold its signature from the Chattanooga
agreement for the time being.[22]

The three-month status quo agreement did not mention
the thorny problem of PWA allotments, and a good deal of
confusion resulted from the omission. Had Administrator
Ickes been invited to the White House meeting, some of this
confusion might have been avoided. Ickes, seldom reluctant
to extend his own influence, had asked to be invited, but
Roosevelt denied the request, probably because he already
had too many cooks working on the power pool.[23] The question now arose between TVA and C & S of whether the standstill agreement implied a suspension of PWA allotments in
the Tennessee Valley, or whether they could proceed freely.
Wehle, who as mediator wanted above all to keep the peace,
proposed a temporary halt to PWA grants and loans, as an
earnest of the government's good faith. TVA's Chairman
Arthur Morgan agreed, writing that the standstill "should
be treated as an effort toward a meeting of minds, and not as
a technical sparring for position . . . the natural inferences
of the agreement should be observed." Willkie, delighted at
this support from Wehle and Morgan, declared that "of course"
they were right. Lilienthal, the most important government
conferee, disagreed vehemently with the Wehle-Morgan
viewpoint. Increasingly fearful of losing control to outsiders,
he privately called Wehle a "horner-in" and wrote Ickes
denouncing Wehle's suggestion that the government should
suspend PWA grants and loans. "While there is, in fact, no
such commitment, the tacit acceptance of a statement to the
contrary might conceivably give rise to a commitment by the
mere fact of acquiescence."[24]

The truth was that although Ickes did not attend the conference, and the standstill agreement did not refer to PWA, Lilienthal and Ickes could easily have worked out an informal suspension had they so desired. They did not, despite the obvious point that such a gesture would have improved the atmosphere of the truce and, more important, of the expected future pooling negotiations. The whole affair now degenerated into a petty squabble over jurisdiction and details of the negotiations, and Wehle, an honest broker, became disgusted with the whole business. His efforts at mediation met with juvenile responses. The truce was not working. And in the middle of the standstill agreement the Public Works Administration allotted over $3 million to Memphis and $660,000 to Jackson, Tennessee, earmarked for new power systems to be connected with TVA transmission lines.[25]

In the meantime, Roosevelt won the election over Landon by the greatest plurality in American history, and government officials now saw less reason than ever to cooperate with the private tradition. Norris exploded against any kind of negotiation with TVA's "enemies." Commonwealth and Southern, he wrote Roosevelt, was "an outfit you know would destroy you in a moment, if they had the power, without regard to the means if they were sure they would not be discovered." During the election campaign Willkie's companies had resorted "to anything which, in their madness, they thought might injure either one of us." Though Louis Wehle claimed to represent Roosevelt, his ideas "were incited and were proposed, in reality, to help the Commonwealth and Southern." "For God's sake," Norris urged Roosevelt, "do not give our laurels of victory to those whom we have defeated." From several sides Roosevelt received strong advice to reject the power pool. His public power allies in Congress had warned against pooling even before the White House meeting of September 30. Congressman Rankin was organizing an anti-pool "public power bloc" in the House. Grassroots protests began to emanate from Chattanooga and elsewhere—rumor attributed them to Lilienthal's influence—and Norris, Roosevelt, and others began to receive popular resolutions opposing the pool.[26]

Just after Lilienthal's reappointment in May 1936, an event heralded by utility men as a signal of a stiffening of New Deal power policy, nineteen southern power companies had entered a broad constitutional lawsuit against TVA. Five of Willkie's companies were among the nineteen. Still pending when the pooling conferences began, this litigation represented a stumbling block to broad cooperation. In principle it resembled the question of PWA allotments, but with the positions occupied by TVA and C & S reversed. Wehle, promoting peace in both cases, tried to persuade Willkie to delay the lawsuit during the negotiating period. Willkie said that it was beyond his control because only five of the plaintiff companies were his. Playing both sides of the street, Willkie told Lilienthal that he would delay the litigation if TVA would delay its construction of dams, a proposition Lilienthal rejected out of hand.[27]

In the midst of the truce period, the nineteen companies pressed their case and obtained from federal district judge John J. Gore a sweeping preliminary injunction that utterly paralyzed TVA's expansion program. At one stroke the Gore injunction reversed the complexion of the power pool negotiations. On the defensive before, Willkie now had secured in court what he could not obtain through bargaining—complete territorial protection from TVA.

Lilienthal responded with typical aggressiveness. Although he knew that Willkie had promised nothing with respect to this litigation, he now wrote Roosevelt that the injunction was a "breach of faith" with the government and with the president personally. The pooling negotiations, therefore, should "be discontinued until the injunction is dissolved." Despite strenuous efforts by Wehle, Sachs, and Willkie, Roosevelt went along with Lilienthal, and the power pool died a quick death. It was never resurrected, even though an appellate court five months afterward ordered the Gore injunction vacated.[28]

Hearing rumors of a scuttle, Willkie affected deep shock: "For me to believe this would be to believe the charges made when the President called the original conference, viz., that his object in calling the conference was political strategy."[29] It was not. The injunction changed Roosevelt's mind because, breach of faith or not, it ruined the government's negotiating position. Almost none of the president's public power allies in Congress had liked the pool in the first place, and they had steadily increased pressure for a discontinuation. Within the government, Lilienthal had turned against the pool three months before the Gore injunction and had vigorously lobbied against it. The Federal Power Commission's vice-chairman, Basil Manly, who had been favorably disposed toward the pool, agreed that the injunction called for reprisal. REA Administrator Morris L. Cooke, an early supporter of pooling, grew less enthusiastic after the Morgan memorandum and even less so after the injunction. That left only Sachs, Wehle, Willkie, and Morgan in favor of a power pool despite the injunction. After this judicial insult, none of these men had much influence with President Roosevelt.

The lineup of supporters and opponents of the power pool disclosed a split within the New Deal between those who viewed the power question as a death struggle between the public and private traditions, and those who wanted to bring cheap electricity to as many citizens as possible, irrespective of public or private ownership. In the first category were Norris, Rankin, La Follette, and other congressmen who, convinced of the continued depravity of all utility magnates, wanted the New Deal to go on punishing them. In the administrative agencies this category included Ickes of PWA and Lilienthal of TVA.

Lilienthal was a true believer in the idea of an "Electrified

America." But after three years of painful negotiations with Willkie, he felt with greater conviction than ever that gains had to come in spite of the private tradition, not in cooperation with it. Wishing to keep a tight personal rein, Lilienthal was profoundly alarmed by the apparent growth during the negotiating period of the Sachs-Wehle-Morgan-Manly influence on Roosevelt. Lilienthal believed TVA to be on the verge of victory over C & S. Like Norris, he recoiled from giving TVA's laurels "to those whom we have defeated." Rejecting the symbolic and substantive compromise represented by the power pool, Lilienthal wished instead to nurture public animus against utilities until the final victory.

The supporters of the pool, by contrast, believed peace must precede progress. Arthur Morgan hated social conflict, deplored the antibusiness rhetoric of the 1936 campaign, and wanted to return to the cooperative spirit exemplified by the National Recovery Administration. He believed political agitation distorted the true meaning of the TVA, and correctly regarded some of the ostensible proponents of unified river development as opportunistic utility haters who cared little for the conservation movement.

Basil Manly believed that despite the obvious dangers of compromise with the private tradition, the economic advantages of pooling were too great to ignore. Power grids in the Tennessee Valley and elsewhere, he wrote Norris after the Gore injunction, "would make electric energy available throughout great regions," and would "expand the rural electrification program at a far more rapid rate than would otherwise be possible."[30]

The great proponent of rural electrification, Morris L. Cooke, approved of the pool in principle. His own experience in trying to secure public and private cooperation in REA paralleled Morgan's efforts in TVA, although Cooke favored Lilienthal over Morgan in most matters of policy. A management engineer and early disciple of Frederick Winslow Taylor, Cooke wanted a peaceful test-demonstration of pooling in the Tennessee Valley, for future application in grids throughout the country.

Alexander Sachs also focused on the pool's great economic potential. Deploring Lilienthal's behavior, he complained to Roosevelt that "the resort by the zealots to coercive and confiscatory tactics" ignored the "social purposes to be served" and undercut "both the ends and the methods of political democracy." Thus the power companies lost an opportunity "to take advantage of the lowest cost money in our financial history." And the economy as a whole suffered from the industry's reluctance to undertake new construction.[31]

The split among Roosevelt's advisers paralleled a split in the president's own mind. He ardently wanted both widespread electrification and complete business recovery. But the power magnates were invaluable political enemies against whom he could rant with profit and impunity. Besides, at the very time Roosevelt had made a generous peace offering, Willkie had procured the insulting Gore injunction, "the like of which," Lilienthal wrote the president, "as far as I know, has never been granted against the Federal Government."[32] It was a slap in Roosevelt's face not only by the private power tradition but also by the judicial branch of the government, and could hardly have diminished his growing resolve to do something about the judiciary. Just six weeks after Judge Gore handed down his decree against TVA, Roosevelt sent Congress a set of long-germinating recommendations for judicial reorganization that set off a national upheaval over "court packing."

For the power pool itself, the fairest verdict is that it was the right idea at the wrong time. An excellent solution to several different economic problems, it failed because of an atmosphere so overheated that genuine compromise appealed to neither side.

6

LIVING IN
THE COURTS

LIKE THE JANUARY 4 CONTRACT, the power pool fell victim to a lawsuit, and TVA's second major venture at cooperation with the private tradition ended in failure. The British Grid, Franklin D. Roosevelt wrote in 1936, showed what benefits could come from such cooperation, "but then, the Britishers do not everlastingly rush to the Supreme Court but instead sit round the table with the Government in good faith—and get results." American utilities, concentrating their fire on TVA, PWA, and the Public Utility Holding Company Act, instituted a mass of litigation that threatened by its very volume to tie up the federal power program in a hopeless tangle of judicial red tape. "Almost from the beginning," a TVA official ruefully observed in 1938, "we have been living in the courts, and have suffered from everything such a status implies."[1]

In the fall of 1934 the Edison Electric Institute commissioned and published a legal opinion pronouncing the TVA "palpably unconstitutional." Regarded by the press as the opening gun in a war against the New Deal power program, the opinion was the handiwork of James M. Beck and Newton D. Baker, two eminent constitutional lawyers. For their efforts the institute paid them $35,000. Beck, a former congressman and solicitor general, was an archconservative whose judgment of the TVA came as no surprise. Baker, Wendell Willkie's idol in the early twenties, was a Wilsonian Democrat who had seriously contended for his party's presidential nomination in 1932. Already he had developed deep qualms about the New Deal, though he voted for Roosevelt a second time in 1936 and remained a Democrat until his death a year later. Both he and Beck would play major roles in the impending litigation against public power.[2]

Before publication of the opinion, Roosevelt heard about it, and in a "My dear Newton" letter wrote Baker that "if the utilities want to get into real trouble with the Congress and the public they will start a fight—and such a fight can only hurt them and their stockholders. As an actual practical fact it cannot succeed." The president asked Baker's help in preventing such "suicide," but the attorney went ahead with his legal opinion.[3]

Armed with the Baker-Beck document, president Thomas N. McCarter of the Edison Electric Institute now presented a "memorial" to Roosevelt asking the government's cooperation in an early test case against the TVA. Chairman Frank McNinch of the Federal Power Commission, to whom Roosevelt referred the inquiry, returned a blistering reply: "In all the history of the American Government no parallel for such a proposal can be found." McCarter was making the astounding suggestion, wrote McNinch, that the government "cast doubt upon the validity of its own legislation."[4]

Thus rebuffed, the private power companies embarked on a systematic attack on Roosevelt's program in courts throughout the country. By 1937, ninety-two suits had been entered against PWA allotments for power projects, fifty-eight against the Securities and Exchange Commission challenging the Public Utility Holding Company Act, and thirty-four against the TVA.[5] The high financial and political stakes in this litigation could be gauged by the eminence of the lawyers who conducted it. Besides Baker and Beck, the utilities hired such leaders of the American bar as John W. Davis and Dean

Acheson. The government responded with an equal array of talent, which besides the excellent staffs of the TVA and the Justice Department included such men as Jerome Frank, Paul Freund, Abe Fortas, and John Lord O'Brian.

For the private tradition, appeal to the courts followed a long-standing pattern. For many years the companies had applied to the judiciary for relief from the rulings of state commissions. They now sought relief from acts of Congress as well. Their basic strategy was to delay the execution of Roosevelt's program until they could either help defeat him in an election or generate enough support in Congress to overturn his policy. In the litigation itself the utilities had practically no success in appellate courts, but they did secure a very large number of temporary injunctions and restraining orders which delayed construction of PWA-funded plants, fulfillment of TVA contracts, and enforcement of holding company legislation. Through electric bills and taxes, the public paid the huge cost of both the attack and the defense.

For the TVA alone, General Counsel James Lawrence Fly calculated that losses aggregated more than a half-million dollars for legal and staff expenses, and more than $5 million in lost revenues from electric sales. For customers denied TVA service, the price differential between private and public rates totalled about $7.7 million. "But greater than any money damages," said Norris on the Senate floor, " ... is the injury to the morale, the organization, the employees, the municipalities that are interested, and the thousands of consumers of electricity who must suffer. ..."[6]

The proportions of the attack caught TVA by surprise. When the first challenge broke in the summer of 1934, the Authority's tiny legal staff did not even have sufficient stenographic help or an adequate law library. But Lilienthal responded quickly. For the now-crucial post of general solicitor (later general counsel) he hired James Lawrence Fly, a Texan who had graduated from the Naval Academy and the Harvard Law School and then served in a Wall Street firm and the

Justice Department. Like Lilienthal he had studied under
Felix Frankfurter at Harvard, and he in turn recruited such
additional young Frankfurter students as Herbert Marks and
Melvin Siegel. A superb administrator, Fly quickly built a
staff worthy in every respect of the formidable opposition it
faced from private utility companies. For the upcoming
constitutional litigation his chief trial lieutenants were
William Fitts, a native Alabaman who earned a Yale law
degree in 1929; and, as a consultant, John Lord O'Brian, an
influential New York Republican and a nationally known
constitutional lawyer.

Oddly, it was not the utilities who first challenged TVA, but
twenty-three coal and twenty-four ice companies, who in
June 1934 petitioned a federal court to enjoin the Authority
from carrying out its power program. They alleged that the
program was unconstitutional and that irreparable injury
would ensue if TVA electricity replaced coal in heating,
hydro power replaced coal-fired steam power, and refrigerators
replaced iceboxes. This ill-conceived, almost Luddite complaint ignored the presumption in favor of technological
advance characteristic of American courts since the Charles
River Bridge case of the 1830s. The companies' attorney, an
astute Birmingham Liberty Leaguer named Forney Johnston,
advised them that the attack on TVA should come from
interests more plausibly threatened—from the power companies, who could more easily establish standing to sue. The
coal and ice litigation never reached trial. Johnston himself
stayed in the fight, becoming the principal attorney in the
impending Ashwander trial.[7]

The first of three great constitutional challenges to TVA's
power program began on September 13, 1934, when George
Ashwander and thirteen other holders of the Alabama Power
Company's preferred stock filed suit in an Alabama court to
enjoin the company from executing the January 4 contract.
The group, comprising only a tiny fraction of the company's

shareholders, circularized all preferred stockholders requesting a contribution of twenty-five cents per share owned to
underwrite the litigation. Later the Edison Electric Institute's entrance into the case as a financial backer ended the
Ashwander group's money problems. The suit itself took the
relatively unusual form of a preferred stockholders' attempt
to prevent the company's management from obeying a contract negotiated by an officer of the parent holding company,
that is, by Wendell Willkie.[8]

The bill of complaint alleged that the transaction of January 4 was illegal because TVA was unconstitutional. On
TVA's motion the case was removed to the United States
District Court for the northern district of Alabama. It there
came before Judge W.I. Grubb, a distinguished jurist who,
unfortunately for the TVA, opposed on principle most of the
new kinds of federal activity begun by the New Deal.

As the case worked its way toward trial, TVA desperately
sought some way to complete the terms of the January 4
contract, trying first to help the municipalities purchase the
Alabama electric properties involved, then to buy the systems itself, and finally to secure the release of the Chemical
Bank's lien. Just when success appeared imminent, Judge
Grubb handed down his decision. Ruling for the Ashwander
group, he declared the January 4 contract illegal because
the government lacked the constitutional power to engage
in the electric utility business. His decree ordered the contract annulled. It enjoined the Alabama cities from accepting
PWA money for building duplicate systems, and from buying
power from TVA. Judge Grubb held that since the TVA Act
spoke repeatedly of "surplus" power sales (that is, power in
excess of the government's own needs in operating nitrate
plants, construction facilities, and navigation locks), the
Authority could sell only that power produced incidentally
rather than deliberately. Since the January 4 contract contemplated selling electricity generated deliberately to exceed
TVA's own needs, that power lay beyond the scope of the

TVA Act. "It is not a surplus," said Judge Grubb, and "it is not to be attributable to any constitutional power."[9]

TVA lost the case, but for several reasons the decision did not signify a complete disaster. First, the court rejected plaintiffs' contention that Willkie signed the January 4 contract under duress. Despite PWA's activity, said Judge Grubb, no duress existed. The contract was unlawful on other grounds: the company lacked the power to sell its transmission lines because TVA lacked the power to buy them. Second, even though the judge did not accept TVA's first line of defense — an argument that the stockholders lacked standing to sue — he did accept, in effect, the Authority's narrow definition of the issue. Deliberately avoiding the troublesome problem of the power program as a whole, TVA's lawyers successfully confined the issue to the constitutionality of Wilson Dam and the January 4 contract. Third, Judge Grubb granted much of what TVA had purported to prove during the trial. In cases certain to be appealed, findings of fact hold particular importance, and Judge Grubb's findings helped the Authority's lawyers build their subsequent arguments.[10]

TVA immediately took the case to the United States Circuit Court of Appeals for the Fifth Circuit. Assuming that the plaintiffs had standing, the appellate court limited its consideration to the constitutionality of Wilson Dam and the issue of "surplus" power. On these narrow points, it reversed Judge Grubb and found for the TVA.[11]

On the stockholders' appeal of the circuit court's decision, the Supreme Court split three ways. As Senator (and future Associate Justice) Sherman Minton interpreted the decision to a national radio audience, it was "a sort of triple threat opinion. You may run with the Chief Justice, pass with Mr. Justice Brandeis, or kick with Mr. Justice McReynolds." Brandeis, supported by Stone, Cardozo, and Roberts, held that the stockholders lacked standing. The Court he declared, should hesitate to decide important constitutional questions brought by stockholders' suits. Furthermore, preferred stockholders like George Ashwander have a more difficult task in showing irreparable injury than do common stockholders, who have equity in the company. Most of all, said Brandeis in a classic statement of a well-known rule, the Court should avoid addressing the constitutional issue if the case could be decided on other grounds.[12]

But Brandeis's was a minority opinion in the Ashwander case. The other five members of the Court ruled that the stock-holders had standing to sue, hence the case must be decided on its merits. Brandeis and his supporters then joined in an 8–1 decision (McReynolds dissenting) in favor of the TVA. For the majority, Chief Justice Hughes held the construction of Wilson Dam constitutional under the commerce and general welfare clauses, and, taking "judicial notice of the international situation at the time the Act of 1916 was passed," under the war power as well. The dam being constitutional, the government could dispose of its property — electric energy created by the dam — irrespective of whether it was generated deliberately or incidentally. Such disposition "must be one adopted in the public interest as distinguished from private or personal ends"; the Alabama Power Company "has no constitutional right to insist that it shall be the sole purchaser of the energy generated at Wilson Dam; that the energy shall be sold to it or go to waste." Explicitly confining its decision to Wilson Dam, said the Court, "we express no opinion" of the other TVA dams or other contracts for the disposition of power. The way thus remained clear for future challenges by the utilities, and they wasted no time in going right back into court.[13]

Even so, both TVA and President Roosevelt scored a mighty triumph in the Ashwander case, one of the tiny number of important pro-New Deal decisions by the Court before 1937. Roosevelt had expected to win, but Lilienthal could hardly believe the good news. "I had completely resigned myself to a bad decision, only holding out hope that we would have some crumb of comfort in that unlike AAA and NRA we would not be swept completely out to sea, bag and baggage." The decision vindicated not only the TVA, but Lilienthal himself, "because my personal character and standards of conduct were raised in the case as a definite issue, and paraded in the brief and in the oral arguments."[14]

That TVA won the appeal did not mean it escaped tangible injury. Judge Grubb's injunction, combined with Willkie's maddening delays in executing the January 4 contract, severely restricted TVA's power business during its first two years of existence. Permitted to sell only a small fraction of its electricity, the Authority lost the revenues it might have had from selling the remainder.

Willkie himself heatedly denied any connection with the case. "I say to you," he wired the White House, "that any such statement made to you by anybody is an absolute and unqualified falsehood and readily demonstrable as such." Yet Willkie served on the board of directors of the Edison Electric Institute, which had entered the Ashwander case in a major way, contributing first $50,000 and eventually more than $100,000 to the plaintiffs' attorneys. Of the total, $78,000 went to Forney Johnston's law firm and $25,000 to James M. Beck, who made the oral argument before the Supreme Court. Willkie, whose company technically stood with TVA as a codefendant, was absent from the directors' meeting which produced the decision to finance the case, and he asked to go on record as "opposed to this motion."[15] Whether he actually did oppose it or objected merely for the record was hard to tell. Perhaps a really strong stand by Willkie could have changed the board's decision. Even at this early date he enjoyed a high standing within the industry, and of course he himself had negotiated the points at issue in the case.

A more solid charge against Willkie derived from the Alabama Power Company's last-minute filing of a brief seeking to invalidate its own contract. This action, wrote Lilienthal, "would shock the conscience of any lawyer who understands the obligations of a codefendant." Whether or not Willkie instigated the brief, he certainly acquiesced in it. For Lilienthal the point was that Willkie, who in speeches and in print repeatedly cited the January 4 contract as evidence of his cooperation with TVA, in fact did everything in his power to frustrate the contract.[16]

TVA itself had not been idle during the tedious appeals of the case. After the hostile lower court ruling the Authority's board of directors went to Congress requesting amendments which would empower TVA to issue bonds for purchasing existing electric systems and more clearly delineate its constitutional power to engage in a utility business. These amendments, though not absolutely vital to the program, helped materially in the appeals of the pending Ashwander case. TVA specifically designed some of the amendments as curative legislation to validate points at issue in the litigation. "If we had courts and attorneys and enemies who were fair," said Norris, "we should not need this amendment." Though it passed in modified form, the legislation had rough going in Congress. On the floor of the House, Andrew Jackson May of Kentucky, one of TVA's harshest enemies, contended that for Congress to pass laws directly affecting pending constitutional cases violated the principle of separation of powers among the branches of the government. Though he strained the point, no one could deny that TVA and its supporters would go to the limits of legal propriety, if not beyond, to escape judicial assassination. The Authority's behavior in this instance foreshadowed even bolder self-defense later, in the second great constitutional case.[17]

The utility companies themselves, not a few disgruntled stockholders, started the second round of litigation. Five of Willkie's companies participated. Known variously as the "nineteen companies," "eighteen companies" (one having withdrawn), and "TEPCO" case, its broad constitutional allegations challenged TVA's existence even more directly than had the Ashwander case.

The TEPCO suit began on May 29, 1936, three months after the Ashwander decision, eleven days after Lilienthal's reappointment, and four months before the White House conference on power pooling. After the denial of several motions to dismiss, hearings began on December 11, 1936, in the middle of the pool negotiations. On December 14, Judge John J. Gore issued his sweeping temporary injunction freezing the TVA power program. Except for certain construction already begun, the Authority could extend neither its service area nor its power lines. It could start no new construction.[18]

Congressman Rankin proposed to impeach Judge Gore. "They have developed," he angrily wrote Norris, "what might be called a 'Judicial Fascisti' in this country, and are trying to govern us by injunction." The Gore decree caused Roosevelt to scuttle the power pool, and impeded TVA's progress for six months. Then the Circuit Court of Appeals for the Sixth Circuit ordered it vacated. Such an injunction, said the appellate court, was an inappropriate method for limiting a federal project under broad constitutional challenge. The circuit court remanded the case to the district for trial, an order that normally would have returned it to Judge Gore. TVA and its friends in Congress had other plans, however, oddly connected with the most important and sensational political event of 1937.[19]

As the Gore injunction went into the appellate process, the country went into an uproar over President Roosevelt's proposal to pack the Supreme Court. This powerful drama split the Democratic party, undercut the New Deal majority in Congress, and cost the president incalculable public support and confidence. The defection of such consistent Roosevelt allies as Herbert Lehman, Tom Connally, and Joseph O'Mahoney measured the country's reaction to the idea of tampering with one of the chief symbols of American constitutional government. Senator Norris, as upset as anyone over the judiciary's obstructionism, asked himself privately what his response would have been if "Harding had offered this bill," and backed Roosevelt only with extreme reluctance.[20]

An inconspicuous eddy of the court fight, practically unnoticed by contemporary reporters, directly influenced the pending TEPCO case. The fiasco over court packing ended formally in the Judiciary Act of 1937. A seemingly innocuous measure in comparison with Roosevelt's original plan, the act merely instituted a few procedural reforms designed to expedite appeals of constitutional judgments by inferior courts. It amounted to little more than a footnote to the upheaval over the president's great scheme. For the TVA it meant a great deal more. The Authority's lawyers, in fact, tailored one section of the bill to fit the circumstances of the pending TEPCO suit. Section 3 of the Judiciary Act required that three judges, not one, must rule on applications for injunctive relief in constitutional cases like TEPCO. The new law thus rescued TVA from Judge Gore and set up a three-judge panel to hear the case on remand from the circuit court. TVA's lawyers drafted an early version of this statute, and General Counsel Fly later claimed to have "actively aided and advised in the amendments to the judiciary bill" designed to prevent "impulsive and prejudicial injunctions by individual judges." Fly lobbied in Washington with Senators McKellar, Black, and McCarran, and with his friend and fellow Texan Hatton Summers, who chaired the House Judiciary Committee.[21]

This episode demonstrated anew TVA's resourcefulness in defense of its interests. No rule or custom prevents an agency's sponsorship of self-serving legislation. Congressman May's objections notwithstanding, the amendments TVA designed to meet the Ashwander crisis followed precedents long accepted, though seldom celebrated, in American politics. Furthermore, something clearly had to be done about the constitutional rulings of individual federal district judges, who had already issued many hundreds of injunctions against various New Deal laws. The Judiciary Act of 1937 met this need. But in its application to the pending TEPCO suit, by no coincidence the first case to come under it, the new law was a well-disguised court-packing measure, as its authors had intended.

The case reached trial in the winter of 1937–1938. With Judge Gore dissenting, as expected, the three-judge panel ruled by 2–1 vote in favor of the Authority. The court found no merit in plaintiffs' argument that the chief but hidden purpose of the TVA Act was to set up a power business under the pretense of promoting navigation, flood control, and national defense. TVA's legally built dams, said the court, generated legal electricity, which could "be rightfully disposed of." The court rejected plaintiffs' charges of coercion, fraud, and malice in TVA's power operations, and their accusation of conspiracy between TVA and PWA through enticement of Willkie's customers. Such "cooperative action by two groups of public officials in administering the provisions of two statutes," wrote Judge Florence Allen for the court, "does not constitute conspiracy." Although there might be "substantial future damage" to the utilities, such damage lay beyond legal redress, for TVA had broken no law.[22]

When the companies appealed the court's decision, the Supreme Court ruled 5–2 (McReynolds and Butler dissenting, Reed taking no part, and Black having just taken his seat), that the plaintiffs lacked standing. Justice Roberts wrote for the majority that the companies' nonexclusive local franchises, "while having elements of property, confer no contractual or property right to be free of competition either from individuals, other public utility corporations, or the state or municipality granting the franchise." Any resulting property damage to the companies lay beyond legal remedy. There existed no conspiracy between TVA and PWA.[23]

Since the Supreme Court denied the companies standing to sue, the decision of the three-judge panel remained the broadest and highest constitutional judgment of the TVA. It still remains so. No subsequent legal challenges to the power program have approached the TEPCO case in magnitude or importance.

The third major constitutional threat to the TVA, a threat contemporaneous with the TEPCO case, involved the Authority's invaluable ally, the Public Works Administration. The suits against PWA-funded municipal electric projects, Ickes told Norris in 1936, revealed "a concerted move on the part of power companies of the country to prevent any city from carrying out its desires in this direction."[24]

Among the total of ninety-two cases against PWA nationwide, eleven applied to Tennessee Valley cities. Chief among these eleven was *Alabama Power Company v. Ickes*, in which the company sought to have the administrator enjoined from making loans and grants for the construction of public electric systems in the cities of Florence, Sheffield, Tuscumbia, and Decatur—all in northern Alabama near Muscle Shoals, all planning to distribute TVA power from Wilson Dam. The proposed allotments totalled more than $1 million. On August 2, 1935, the Supreme Court of the District of Columbia granted a preliminary injunction, but two months later dismissed the complaint. The company appealed, and the case was remanded for trial. The trial court, the court of appeals, and the United States Supreme Court all ruled that the Alabama Power Company, lacking exclusive franchises in the cities, lacked standing to sue. If damages resulted from PWA's action they were, as in the TEPCO case, beyond legal remedy.[25]

When at last PWA won its victory in the Supreme Court in the Alabama Power Company and Duke Power Company lawsuits (the latter being the principal test case), a triumphant Harold Ickes crowed over his enemies:

> The lawyers in these cases were smart enough to keep the government in trouble but not wise enough to get business out of trouble. All that they have accomplished for their huge fees is an accumulation of a vast amount of ill will for their clients, the dissipation of perhaps millions of dollars of stockholders' money for legal fees and court costs, delay in the execution of the registered will of the citizens of .many communities ex-

pressed through their local governments, and the flouting of the will of the nation expressed through Congress.

For three years, said Ickes, men, mines, factories, and mills lay idle, and economic recovery was correspondingly delayed. Now the Alabama and Duke decisions would release 100 million man-hours of work.[26]

To Ickes and other public power men it appeared that the private tradition had attempted not merely to attenuate Roosevelt's program but to kill it, even if national recovery suffered in the process. For five exasperating years TVA lived under clouds of constitutional challenge, enduring an uncertain future as well as lost revenues. Not one of the companies' early victories survived on appeal. By 1939 the utilities had exhausted every chance for judicial rescue from the TVA. Willkie now faced Lilienthal with his best ammunition already spent.

7

THE TEPCO SALE
AND PWA

DURING THE LONG PERIOD of legal challenge, TVA's biggest problem was finding new markets for its power. If demand failed to match supply, then Willkie's oft-repeated prediction that TVA was overbuilding the region's electrical capacity would come true, to the acute embarrassment of the New Deal. In the fight of 1935 over amendments to the TVA Act, the Authority had partially lost control over the rate and sequence of its construction. Senator Kenneth D. McKellar of Tennessee, who viewed TVA as a gigantic pork barrel for his state, sometimes used his position on the Senate Appropriations Committee to push the construction schedule faster than TVA's planners wished to go. More and more hydropower thus became available, and by mid-1937 TVA was about to find itself with huge blocks of electricity and no ready market.[1]

After Roosevelt scuttled the power pool, Willkie and Lilienthal could not agree on the terms of a second extension of the January 4 contract, and the contract lapsed for good in February 1937. This closed the convenient market outlet formerly provided by C & S. "While thus cutting off the Authority's revenues from private utilities," an angry Lilienthal wrote the president, "the same companies, by securing injunctions against the Authority and many cities with which the Authority has contracts for power supply, had plainly decided upon *starving out the Authority*."[2]

To meet the problem TVA negotiated a series of sale contracts with the Arkansas Power and Light Company and such industrial firms as the Monsanto Chemical Company, the Victor Chemical Works, and the Aluminum Company of America. Despite protests from Norris, Rankin, and other public power militants that this action violated the preference clause in TVA legislation, Lilienthal really had no alternative. If the Authority did not sell to these nonpreferential customers, it could sell to nobody, and it would lose badly needed revenues at a critical time.[3]

Disposition of electricity to industrial firms worked well as a stopgap, but did nothing to further the public power tradition in the Tennessee Valley. Accordingly, Lilienthal and his staff continued their strenuous efforts to break the logjam of litigation and keep the beleaguered municipalities enthusiastic about TVA and confident of eventual victory. It was a massive endeavor, atomized in scores of towns from one end of the Tennessee River to the other. It required the utmost attention and tact. It involved promoting the Authority through publicity and policies calculated to win local support, lobbying with state assemblies and governors for legislation to facilitate the organization of municipal and cooperative distributors, and negotiating tediously with the newly-established agencies. Success did not come until 1939, when Willkie, defeated in local referenda and in court, and under the immediate threat of competition from PWA-funded public plants, had no choice but to sell.

Lilienthal enjoyed the contest for public opinion, making dozens of speeches up and down the Valley. He constantly reiterated the "electrification of America" theme. He also geared his argument directly to his audience by dwelling on TVA's role in the economic future of the South. And he almost never let pass an opportunity for needling the private tradition. "We are proud," he said in a Memphis speech which recalled the rhetoric of the Populists, to count among our leading enemies the whole Tory crowd concentrated in New York and Chicago that always fights every move toward giving the average man and woman a better chance. The interests of this crew of reactionaries and your interests are diametrically opposed. There is a conflict here that can not be reconciled. Either TVA has to be for you or it has to be for this other crowd. When that crowd begins to sing the praises of TVA, it is time for you to throw us out.[4]

Lilienthal devoted much time to explaining and promoting one of his pet creations, the Electric Home and Farm Authority, a TVA affiliate set up to expedite the appliance-saturation program. EHFA worked with manufacturers for the production of low-cost models and made low-interest loans to consumers toward purchases of stoves, refrigerators, and other appliances. The agency never realized its potential on a national scale, but in the Tennessee Valley it played an important role in the program of loadbuilding essential to justify the low rates. TVA itself built consumer load in almost every conceivable way, including in some areas a house-to-house instruction on how to maximize the benefits of electricity. Immensely pleased with the results, Lilienthal wrote Frankfurter in 1934 that the "campaign to change public opinion on public power has been successful beyond anything I could have asked for in 5 years, much less 5 months."[5] The great jump in usage by residents of the yardstick communities seemed to validate his arguments about public power as well as elasticity of demand.

Lilienthal mailed out "How are we doing?" letters to a random sample of residential power customers, and the response favored TVA twenty to one. A physician who lived near Wilson Dam replied:

The power trust has done more to sap the vitality of the Nation than the hookworm. And I would rather be the most humble worker for the T.V.A. and do all I could for humanity for a few short years and die than to be the whole power trust and wiggle in its hookworm slime for a million years.

Clearly, the campaign to win the allegiance of Valley people had succeeded. "I am having," Lilienthal wrote, "the time of my life."[6]

TVA labored mightily to secure the passage of state legislation making possible the organization of local groups into retailers of its electricity. The Authority's lawyers beat a path to Nashville, Montgomery, and other capitals in a constant lobbying effort before interest groups, legislative committees, and governors. The issue became complicated by TVA's refusal to submit to the jurisdiction of state utility commissions, and by the serious problem of tax-replacement that developed when tax-exempt public agencies displaced private companies. With the help of legislation by Congress, TVA and its local allies overcame these problems at different times in different states. On the whole, TVA won its main objectives everywhere, though the victory did not come easily. Kentucky, the last state involved, did not fall into line until 1942.[7]

Because of the great market stakes at issue, TVA's fight for public power centered in the region's large cities — Knoxville, Memphis, and Chattanooga. In each case the Public Works Administration proved an almost indispensable ally, as it had in a dozen small towns.

No city of its size received so much direct benefit from the Authority as did Knoxville, where the board of directors had set up TVA's headquarters in 1933. The electric utility in Knoxville occupied the last layer of a typical holding company structure, being run by the Tennessee Public Service Company, a subsidiary of National Power and Light, which in turn was a subsidiary of the great holding company, Electric Bond and Share. To get the benefit of TVA's low rates, the citizens of Knoxville in November 1933 voted by a wide margin to turn out the private company and build or purchase a system for public operation. The city offered to buy the existing private plant, but the company refused on the reasonable grounds that a sale would break up its integrated system extending into surrounding counties. Knoxville then applied for a loan and grant from the Public Works Administration, and with Lilienthal's help through a personal appeal to Ickes soon obtained an allotment of $2.6 million. The company then shifted gears, offering either to cut its own rates or to sell or lease its plant to the city—do anything, in short, which would prevent the construction of a competing plant.[8]

When the city and the company failed to settle on a purchase price, TVA stepped in with an offer to buy the properties, including the outlying systems, and then resell the urban facilities to Knoxville. Lilienthal began direct negotiations with C.E. Groesbeck, the head of Electric Bond and Share. As in Lilienthal's numerous negotiations with Willkie, selling price was a question of surpassing importance. On the private side, stockholders' interests were at stake. More significant, price bore an intimate relationship to the national issue of comparative public and private rates. If the private companies sold out at a distress figure, TVA would receive properties carrying a reduced rate base. In consequence, charges to consumers could be reduced, and the experiment in public ownership would succeed automatically. Both sides keenly appreciated this transcendent fact. TVA's use of the Public Works Administration to improve its own bargaining position therefore infuriated the negotiators on the private side, who were caught in a squeeze play engineered by their own government. Groesbeck objected to it as strenuously as had Willkie. Replying in a tone of outraged innocence, Lilienthal wrote Groesbeck:

> You refer to the "activities of the Tennessee Valley Authority in the area" and to the loan and grant to the City of Knoxville by the Public Works Administration very much as if these two agencies were outside interests plotting the destruction of your business. You seem to forget that both the Tennessee Valley Authority and the Public Works Administration are instrumentalities of the people of the United States; that their "activities" which you thus decry are in execution of policies of the entire

nation, formulated under the Constitution by the President and the Congress.[9]

Both sides in Knoxville wanted a sale, however, and after some additional haggling over price, Lilienthal and Groesbeck reached an agreement. At the last moment, a stockholder's suit intervened, as it had in the January 4 contract with Willkie, and the deal was off. Knoxville then announced that it was going ahead with a competing plant, using PWA funds for construction. The company interrupted construction with a series of legal maneuvers, but finally dropped its attack, and on May 20, 1938, accepted the $7.5 million offered jointly by Knoxville and TVA for the properties in and around the city. The system changed hands in September 1938.[10]

Despite the ultimate victory for public power, an exasperating and frustrating period of five years separated the pro-TVA referendum and the conversion to municipal ownership. During the period TVA and Knoxville each believed at various times that the other was not trying hard enough to solve mutual problems. Changes in city government required tedious briefings of newly-elected officials. Other cities competed for the power TVA had allotted to Knoxville, and it was hard to keep the PWA money obligated in the face of continued delays in spending funds which were supposed to be used at once to alleviate unemployment.

The same pattern prevailed with the Memphis utility, another property of Electric Bond and Share. The election, held in the fall of 1934, followed a colorful and acrimonious campaign based in part on the historic enmity between the power company and E. H. Crump, the "Boss" of Memphis. In a full-page advertisement in the *Commercial Appeal*, Crump complained that in past years the "power monopoly" had "spied on me — had detectives to trail me. . . . My personal checks were stolen." He urged his fellow citizens to vote "yes" on the referendum for municipal ownership.[11]

The public tradition scored an even greater victory in Memphis than it had in Knoxville. "We beat the Power Trust

17 to 1," Crump gloated in a letter to Norris. "We now expect them to resort to all court technicalities." And they did. As in Knoxville, litigation held up a sale until the city actually began constructing its own system with the help of a large PWA allotment. The power company then surrendered, and in the summer of 1939 Memphis went into the power business in partnership with TVA. The five years between the referendum and the execution of its mandate witnessed a flow of nervous communication between Memphis officials and TVA, as they worked out their joint strategy. Having been burned in litigation, both parties planned each step carefully, and took great pains to avoid even the appearance of a "conspiracy" among TVA, Memphis, and PWA. A city official, for example, invited Lilienthal to absent himself from the parade and celebration at which Memphis received its first PWA check.[12]

The most important of all the local fights was in Chattanooga, the home of TEPCO and one of the best industrial power markets in the state. "Chattanooga," wrote George Fort Milton, a well-known local newspaper editor and friend of the TVA, "is the core and center of the Tennessee Electric Power Company, really the Hindenburg line of private power." The stakes in the fight involved not just the local utility operation but the whole company, whose lines covered most of the state. Accordingly, the election in Chattanooga was the most bitterly contested of all.[13]

The company did everything it could to win. It lent its advertising manager to a committee of "Citizens and Taxpayers" which did most of its work through TEPCO employees and ground out reams of propaganda opposing public power. Some company officials allegedly paid for votes and dispensed whiskey on election day. Others purchased two ghost lots for the purpose of qualifying as voters 120 nonresident employees of the company. Wendell Willkie, apparently trying to circumvent Tennessee's law prohibiting political contributions by corporations registered in the state, contributed from the treasury of the nonresident Commonwealth and Southern checks totalling $20,000, practically the entire expenses of the "Citizens and Tax-payers" group. This association was investigated by a local grand jury and by the Black committee in Congress, which was inquiring into lobbying in connection with the holding company bill of 1935. The state utilities commission found TEPCO guilty of improper subsidy of a newspaper and of a local business which had joined the fight against public power.[14]

But the public tradition had equally energetic representa-tion in Chattanooga. TVA pointedly took no direct part in the election, but its timely announcement of plans to erect a dam near the city doubtless won votes away from the opposition. For whatever reasons, in March 1935 the citizens of Chattanooga opted for public power by a margin of three to one. The same referendum created the Chattanooga Electric Power Board (an appointive municipal body whose type TVA recommended everywhere), to take charge of negotia-tions for the acquisition of a public system and to operate it once acquired. The vote particularly embarrassed C & S, because Chattanooga was the home of TEPCO, whose antecedents had begun business there shortly after the turn of the century. Furthermore, the company had made note-worthy strides in progressive management in recent months, with its objective rate plan and appliance sales program.

For eighteen months the territorial limitation of the Jan-uary 4 contract kept TVA out of Chattanooga. Negotiations with the Electric Power Board went forward anyway, and a contract was ready when the TVA-C & S agreement expired in November 1936. But the signing of the document was still further delayed, first by Roosevelt's request to put off Chat-tanooga while pooling negotiations went forward, then by the extension of the January 4 contract, and finally by the Gore injunction. City officials watched with anger and frustration as industrial firms preempted TVA power. But the Authority had not forgotten Chattanooga, and signed the contract once the appellate court vacated the Gore injunction.[15]

The city still had no distribution system. As in other towns, the choice lay between constructing its own plant or purchasing the existing one. In line with TVA policy, the Electric Power Board had offered at once to purchase that part of the Tennessee Electric Power Company which served Chattanooga. President Guild of TEPCO returned a haughty rebuff, declaring that for the company to "sell its business in Chattanooga would be taking the hub out of the wheel." He had a valid point. Loss of Chattanooga would cripple the company. But for the power board, whose legal duty was to get the city into the power business, Guild's position left only the alternative of constructing a duplicate system. An appeal to Willkie proved fruitless. Like Guild, he would not even discuss a sale.[16]

While Willkie did nothing, Chattanooga's engineers proceeded to draw blueprints for a new power system. Now, a purchase by TVA of the statewide Tennessee Electric Power Company seemed the obvious solution to the Authority's need for markets and C & S's need to avoid losing Chattanooga, the heart of the company. The series of adverse court decisions had steadily narrowed Willkie's alternatives. And in March 1938 Chattanooga received its first check from the Public Works Administration for construction of a competing electric system. Under the terms of the allotment, which totalled $4.33 million, the money had to be spent by June 30, 1939, a requirement that gave added urgency to the ensuing three-cornered negotiations among Willkie, Lilienthal, and the city's power board. The local issue thus merged into a broader plan for the purchase of TEPCO. In the fall of 1938, PWA allotted an additional $3.3 million, and Willkie faced certain ruin if he did not sell. Chattanooga had already begun to build, although the local board repeatedly offered to halt construction if Commonwealth and Southern would surrender. "You can appreciate," the board pointedly told Willkie, "that each day this construction program advances the value of your properties to the City of Chattanooga becomes progressively less."[17]

With Willkie and Lilienthal alternately gibing at each other in speeches and press releases, the several parts of the Tennessee Valley power fight—litigation, propaganda, and scramble for markets—all seemed to be coming to a head at once. Inside the TVA itself, the Morgan-Lilienthal feud had become a public spectacle.

Chairman Morgan's successive defeats in the Lilienthal reappointment and the power pool convinced him that the New Deal preferred punishing the private tradition to settling the issue fairly. In the aftermath of the power pool scuttle, Morgan began openly to attack Lilienthal's methods of dealing with Willkie, and the feud entered its final crisis. Lilienthal, who incorrectly believed Morgan to be conspiring with Willkie (he complained to Senator La Follette of the "close and skillful team-play which is going on"), fought back with superior resources, and Morgan's departure became only a matter of time.[18]

The chairman was not uncritical of the private tradition and on occasion harshly denounced it himself. He liked to inveigh against "rugged individualism," and enjoyed pointing out that only about half of a customer's electric bill was reasonable, the rest being tribute to the power magnates. "Few Oriental monarchs," said Morgan, "ever had such tribute pouring in upon them." Yet Morgan regarded much of Lilienthal's rhetoric about the private companies and TVA's yardstick as misleading and unfair. TVA's case was so strong anyway, Morgan believed, that such publicity did more harm than good.[19]

Without allies in the administration, Morgan by 1937 had no recourse except to resign or take his case to the public. Unwisely, he decided on the second alternative. In articles for the *New Republic*, the *New York Times*, the *Atlantic Monthly*, and the *Saturday Evening Post*, he denounced such practices as "the incitement of class hatred and development of dramatic political issues on which a few men may ride to public prominence." He spoke boldly of the "improprieties" of the "working policy of the TVA on the power issue." Retaliation to the abuses of the private tradition through the use of "false and misleading propaganda," he wrote, "tends to substitute private dictation for democratic process of government." If the question were settled fairly, he said in unspoken but clear reference to Lilienthal, certain men would be left "without a place in the limelight."[20]

Morgan's indiscreet press campaign finally undid him. President Roosevelt, long reluctant to interfere, now had no choice but to settle the quarrel. It was splitting the TVA internally, blackening its public image, complicating its relationship with Willkie, and causing trouble with its appropriations in Congress.[21] The fight was also hurting the New Deal politically, as Roosevelt's enemies tried to portray Morgan as a martyr. When Morgan indirectly accused his colleagues of dishonesty, the feud became national news, and reporters began to speculate about a new Teapot Dome.

Roosevelt acted quickly now, after procrastinating far too long. Essaying to force Morgan's resignation, the president called all three directors before him in a series of three dramatic White House hearings and insisted that they either substantiate their charges or withdraw them. Morgan thwarted Roosevelt's plan by doggedly refusing to go into detail, insisting instead on an investigation by Congress. His hand forced, Roosevelt on March 23, 1938, fired Morgan outright, citing his "contumacy" and inability to accept a minority role within the board.[22]

The subsequent and widely reported investigation of the TVA by a joint committee of Congress cleared the board majority of wrongdoing, and also provided a comprehensive public scrutiny of every part of the Authority's program. The headline press coverage of the hearings, which went on intermittently from May to December 1938, offered an opportunity for publicity on which the public and private traditions each attempted to capitalize. Prominent appearances by Willkie and by all three members of the TVA board took up much of the committee's time. Their testimony filled a large part of the six thousand-page record of the hearings. In its report the committee's Democratic majority upheld Lilienthal against Morgan and vindicated the TVA, essentially by praising it with faint damns. The committee's Republican minority came to the equally predictable conclusion that the whole program was inefficient and unnecessary. For the TVA itself, the burden of preparing for the investigation brought virtually all other business, including negotiations for the TEPCO sale, to a temporary halt.

For months before the investigation Willkie had offered, in public as well as private, to sell "in their entirety" those parts of his southern companies directly threatened by TVA. But his proposals always contained implied or stated requirements that once the Authority had purchased what it wanted, it must refrain from further competition. Citing the preference clause, Lilienthal consistently refused to yield this point, characterizing Willkie's requirement as an attempt to erect a "Chinese Wall" around the TVA.

Yet by 1938 each side recognized that a straight purchase of TEPCO would best serve the interests of both. TVA desperately needed a market for its rapidly growing power supply. The companies needed a settlement that would preserve their investors' capital from destruction through PWA-financed competition. The Supreme Court's decisions of January 1938, which upheld PWA allotments, made quick action by the companies imperative. In this context of urgency, the long-standing mutual hostility of the Willkie-Lilienthal relationship increased the difficulty of negotiations.[23]

After Willkie had publicly offered to sell, in a press release of January 1938, Lilienthal on March 4 addressed letters to Willkie and to the presidents of the companies involved. He proposed that TVA purchase the entire Tennessee Electric Power Company and small portions of the Alabama and Mississippi Power Companies. The price, Lilienthal wrote, "should be primarily the actual legitimate cost of these properties," less accrued depreciation. Willkie replied that he was "delighted to accept your proposal," but shifted the basis for price to "the purchase of these properties as going concerns"—a formula implying practically no upper limit of value. The two men met in Washington and agreed to undertake the intensive engineering and accounting studies which would yield working figures for a purchase price.

Willkie spoke of the long-term goal of "stabilizing" the situation, by which he meant that TVA, once the deal went through, should refrain from further competition outside the purchased territory. Lilienthal, as always, brought up the "definite and specific obligation under the Tennessee Valley Authority Act" to give preference to public agencies regardless of their location, by which he meant that TVA was not going to agree to stay out of any territory. But this question of a "Chinese Wall," the bone of contention between Lilienthal and Willkie from the beginning, now had less relevance than it had in 1933. Lilienthal admitted as much when he wrote that the amount of power TVA would eventually generate "is known, within narrow limits." Once a market existed "for all of that power, with a reasonable reserve for expansion and increase within the region served, then the situation with respect to the power companies' properties lying outside of such region becomes stabilized." The gist of this statement was that the Authority would have no power to dispose of once the TEPCO area converted to public power. Though TVA could not legally give any self-denying guarantees, the territorial problem would not arise.

With a tacit understanding on this point, both sides now began to calculate a purchase price for the Tennessee Electric Power Company. After three months of study, Willkie's consultants proposed $106 million, Lilienthal's $56.9 million.

Each man pronounced the other's figure outrageous, and the negotiations stalemated. Several weeks passed with no progress whatever. "As I reflected about these two fellows and their conflicting attitudes," recalled L.J. Wilhoite, who was head of Chattanooga's Electric Power Board and directly involved in the negotiation, "I could not help but feel that both were playing a bluffing game buttressed by their angry dislike of each other."[24]

Willkie now suggested arbitration, as he had done earlier in the negotiations. In succession he proposed a board of three arbitrators, one to be named by TVA, one by C & S, and one by the chief justice; then a group of private citizens, one of whom would be Felix Frankfurter; and finally the Securities and Exchange Commission. Lilienthal refused, saying that TVA could not legally delegate its powers. The SEC also declined Willkie's suggestion. To many observers, however, Willkie's position seemed eminently fair, and it received some important newspaper support. Lilienthal stuck to his refusal, and the stalemate continued. The whole negotiation went on in an atmosphere of hostile press releases and public statements by both Lilienthal and Willkie, sensationalism attending the concurrent TVA investigation, and agitation by the Electric Power Board of Chattanooga, which was becoming frantic over the time limit on its PWA allotment.

In the middle of the stalemate, Lilienthal suddenly became violently ill with undulant fever after drinking some unpasteurized milk offered by a friendly Valley farmer. The attack persisted for months, and for a time his doctors thought he might not recover. Forced to withdraw from the negotiation, he turned matters over to a pair of bright young staff members, Joseph Swidler and Julius Krug. Swidler had been a power attorney with TVA almost from the beginning, and had negotiated many of the Authority's early power contracts. Exceptionally quick-witted, he would later serve for a dozen years as TVA's general counsel, and afterward as chairman of both the Federal Power Commission and the New York Public

Service Commission. At the time of the TEPCO negotiations he was thirty-two years old. Krug was even younger. Only thirty-one, he had worked as a utility economist with Lilienthal on the Wisconsin Public Service Commission and later served on the staff of the Federal Communications Commission. Outgoing and likable, he fitted the role of negotiator perfectly. In 1946 President Truman would appoint him Secretary of the Interior.

For a while Swidler and Krug also deadlocked with Willkie over the question of price. But everyone concerned now wanted the deal to go through, and the parties finally agreed on a compromise price of $78 million. The figure meant that TEPCO's bondholders and preferred stockholders would receive one hundred percent of their investment. The common stockholders — in effect C & S, which owned almost all the equity — would receive about $7 million, a price far below what the stock had once been worth but far above what the company might have expected after losing so many referenda and court decisions.

The final agreement came just after the Supreme Court's decision against Willkie in the TEPCO case. The compromise purchase price was therefore widely regarded as a symbolic victory for him even though the sale was a substantive loss. For his budding political career, the deal provided a great boost, and he won the admiration of businessmen everywhere for having driven a hard bargain from an underdog position. TVA's negotiator Julius Krug later testified that the property was not actually worth $78 million "without consideration of what might be termed 'nuisance value,'" which amounted to about $9 million. Though TVA had never before agreed to pay such an excess, said Krug, the company simply would not sell for a lower figure, and the excess was justifiable because it eliminated TVA's competition.[25]

One final hurdle remained. The TVA Act did not authorize the issuance of bonds to purchase existing generating facilities, such as those included in the TEPCO deal. When TVA went to Congress for enabling amendments, its enemies attempted to attach a series of hostile clauses designed to freeze the Authority's area of operations. More serious for the problem at hand, they also tried to tie the bond authorization to the exceedingly complex and controversial question of tax replacement for the states and counties which would suffer from the transfer from private to public operation of the power business. Only the parliamentary skill of Norris and a few well-chosen words by President Roosevelt prevented Congress from talking the bill to death, or at least delaying its passage until Chattanooga's PWA allotment expired.

But at last, on August 15, 1939, Lilienthal and Willkie made the transfer. In a ceremony which took up the entire sixth floor of a New York bank, Willkie accepted the government's check for the transmission and generating facilities and the cities' payments for distribution systems. "I had a strange sensation:" Lilienthal wrote afterward. "It was much like the experience that they say a drowning man has of having his whole past life go through his mind in a few seconds." Willkie, seldom at a loss for words, said "Thanks, Dave. This is a lot of money for a couple of Indiana farmers to be kicking around. For this," said Willkie, handing Lilienthal a sheaf of irrelevant papers, "I give you the deeds of the Tennessee Electric Power Company."[26] Several hundred persons watched as newsreel cameramen recorded the elaborate climax of the long drama. The film played in theaters across the country in the late summer of 1939 and again during the presidential campaign of 1940.

Off camera, Willkie was less affable. He had sold out, he said in a press statement, at a loss and "with regret." His own injury, however, "will not be in vain if it serves to arouse the American people against government invasion of their business." Willkie bought full-page signed advertisements in a dozen major newspapers, attacking the forced sale and predicting insuperable tax-replacement problems for Tennessee and many of its counties. "To our numerous friends and associates in Tennessee," wrote Willkie, "many of whom have been most helpful and considerate, we are deeply indebted and very grateful. We wish them every success. Our hope is they will never be required to defend a business of their own against government subsidized competition."[27] Lilienthal replied in similar spirit, and the old argument, now stripped of practical basis, went on as if by unbreakable habit.

The long-standing question of territorial restriction — of the "Chinese Wall" around the Authority's area of service — automatically disappeared, at least as a major problem, when TVA acquired a market for all its electricity. "We closed our dispute with the Tennessee Valley Authority," wrote the head of the Alabama Power Company, "with the definite feeling that TVA would confine its operations" to the territory transferred in 1939.[28] The Authority now had exclusive markets in practically all of Tennessee and in large portions of northern Alabama and northeastern Mississippi. The legal possibility for further encroachment remained for twenty years. But despite an immense and mainly unforeseen growth of TVA's productive capacity, the Authority confined itself, with a few exceptions, to the area it served in 1940.

TVA might not have won its fight for urban markets without the help of the Public Works Administration. In city after city the same drama unfolded, as if played by an itinerant group of actors touring the Tennessee Valley. First, a city would vote to go into the power business.[29] Then it would offer to purchase the existing utility, and the private company would decline the price offered. Next, the city would secure financing from PWA to augment its own bond issues. After intervening litigation it would threaten to build, or actually begin to build a competing system which if finished would bankrupt the private company. Finally, the company would sell at a compromise price. As Willkie put it, "In effect the Government holds a gun to the head of the utility and says, 'Sell at our price or we will duplicate.'" For the municipalities voting on the question of public power, said Willkie, it was a case of "heads I win and tails you lose," because once PWA money flowed in the city was certain to come out ahead. "When it got at the point where the cities were actually going up the city streets, building duplicate distribution lines," said Willkie, "and the Supreme Court had said that they would not pass on the constitutionality of the question, then I became a realist."[30]

8

A SUCCESSFUL BUT UNREPEATED EXPERIMENT

BY 1939 TVA had won all its lawsuits and had secured a large, integrated territory for its yardstick. Its power program was a healthy going concern, well prepared for a great leap forward in production for the impending war emergency. Few other public agencies, if any, matched TVA's reputation for overall efficiency. This broad success derived not only from Lilienthal's substantive victory over Willkie, but also from TVA's outstanding performance in a thousand details of its job, and from an intensive, deliberate appeal to the public.

Completely successful in its effort to sell itself to the Valley, TVA never realized its concurrent aim of capturing the allegiance of the nation as well. Willkie and the private tradition lost the battle for the Tennessee Valley; but they won a qualified victory in the war against public power and valley authorities elsewhere. As TVA entered the 1940s its own reputation remained high, but it was still *sui generis*. This paradox—that TVA, though successful, was never duplicated—resulted in part from the private tradition's own exertions, but even more from changing political conditions and opposition to the TVA idea within the government itself.

In its fight for the loyalty of the Valley, TVA's insuperable advantage was its status as an agency spending great sums of money locally during a national economic depression. Most regions, regardless of their politics, are not in the habit of banishing lucrative federal projects. Yet TVA's programs, grafted onto an already complex federal system, still created a host of problems. The agricultural effort required the consent and cooperation of farmers. Building dams necessitated relocation of schools and churches, removal of families from ancestral homesites, rerouting of roads, condemnation of farms, and inundation of tax-producing real estate. The power program demanded local efforts in public power referenda and in the construction or purchase of distribution systems.

TVA promoted its own acceptance by deliberately absorbing as many local agencies as possible into the execution of its program. This "grass roots" policy was a brainchild of Harcourt Morgan, who liked to talk about "the integration of natural and human resources," and once told President Roosevelt that "Democracy is achieved from the bottom up." David Lilienthal, the chief apostle of the idea, devoted much of his well-known book *TVA: Democracy on the March* to an exposition and glorification of it:

> Decentralizing the administration of government functions that are clearly national has been carried so far in this valley that it is literally true (I can think of no exceptions) that, whenever there is a state or a local institution which can perform part of the task that has been assigned by law to the TVA, TVA has sought to have that non-federal agency do it.[1]

The grass roots policy helped gain consensus acceptance of the TVA, but the policy had a negative side, too. In agriculture, it meant working through the system of land-grant colleges, with which Harcourt Morgan had been associated for forty years. Morgan's critics later pointed out that this decision implied a program of limited objectives whose practical effect was that while TVA's efforts succeeded on their own terms, they did not go to the root of the problems of poor farmers, who were the vast majority in Valley agriculture. TVA actually adopted a hostile attitude toward other New Deal ventures in agriculture, such as the Soil Conservation Service and the tenant-oriented Farm Security Administration.

The grass roots policy also meant acquiescing in white supremacy. In general, Negroes received short shrift from the TVA, as they did from many other New Deal agencies. Black agricultural colleges had no role in TVA's fertilizer program. Construction villages such as the model town of Norris housed white families only. TVA obviously had a ticklish problem here, as a new federal agency thrust into the South. But it also had a unique opportunity to ameliorate the racial situation. It made little effort to do so, despite repeated protests from the NAACP over Jim Crowism and abuses of black workers by white foremen. TVA did strive to employ Negroes in the proportion of their population in the Valley, about 10 percent, but most of its black workers were unskilled laborers or orderlies. "In short," wrote two investigators in *The Crisis*, "no attempt is made at educating the Negro or diversifying his skills; the T.V.A. aims to maintain the *status quo*."[3]

Insofar as the grass roots idea applied to electric power, it meant promoting the organization of local cooperative and municipal distributorships. For rural cooperatives the argument had some validity. Voluntary groups engaged in erecting electric systems to serve their own farms contrasted strikingly with the private power tradition's apathetic approach to rural electrification. TVA and its cooperatives sometimes battled the private companies in the countryside, racing to beat the construction of "spite lines." With these lines, which paralleled routes proposed for serving a rural cooperative, the companies aimed to preempt the area's electric business and ruin the cooperative's chances of success. Yet once the cooperatives began operations and farmers had electric service, the urgency of broad citizen participation evaporated. At annual membership meetings, some cooperatives had trouble meeting the requirements for a 5 percent quorum.[4]

For its municipal distributors, TVA advised that local power boards such as that in Chattanooga be appointive, not elective—good sense, perhaps, but hardly implying faith in democracy from the bottom up. Once the boards went to work, TVA wielded essentially dictatorial powers, controlling both the pricing and financial policies of its satellites. The Authority wisely protected its low rates by removing the irrestible temptation for cities to use municipal utility revenues to augment taxes in paying the general expenses of local government. A firm central policy was also necessary to weld more than a hundred local distributors into a unified power system. But it was hardly grass roots democracy, as Lilienthal suggested when he told a group of Valley power distributors that TVA's methods were "the twentieth-century equivalent of the eighteenth-century Town Meeting." TVA's management of its power system was probably no more democratic than Commonwealth and Southern's. "A suggestion today," a careful student wrote in 1969 of the relationship between TVA and its municipal distributors, "that TVA's power operations have increased citizens' participation or have encouraged anything resembling a town meeting would evoke laughter anywhere in the Valley."[5] Perhaps the Authority created an impression of participation, and thereby stimulated morale, as it claimed to do with the project as a whole. But actually the grass roots rhetoric had little factual basis in TVA's power program. The idea itself is mostly irrelevant to the electric utility business, once a community has made its basic decision for or against public power.

In regional planning, grass roots democracy meant playing down or abandoning the broad scale approach envisioned by President Roosevelt and attempted by Chairman Morgan. Complaints against Morgan's plans plagued TVA in its early months, and Senator McKellar boasted in 1941 that only his efforts on the Senate Appropriations Committee had kept the Authority to what he regarded as its central objective—dam building—rather than half-cocked schemes "to uplift the ignorant and benighted people of the Tennessee Valley." Actually the board majority had little faith in Morgan's version

of planning anyway, and greatly feared the adverse local reaction to his unfettered ideas.[6] Accordingly, they sharply circumscribed his influence at the start and practically dropped
planning altogether after his departure. Yet most of TVA's
specific programs, when given a fair chance, did succeed.
Library and educational experiments, stimulation of small
Valley industries, training programs for construction workers,
and most of all the superbly designed model town of Norris
attracted the admiration of scores of old progressives and new
city and regional planners. TVA never came close to fulfilling
Morgan's hopes, however, and from about 1935 onward was
chiefly an electric utility and a river-control agency.

Confining itself to these functions, TVA completely succeeded on its own terms. Its full development and control of
the river for power, navigation, and flood control became a
model, envied and widely emulated abroad. In the United
States public policy never completely adopted the multiple-
purpose idea, even during the New Deal. The Flood Control
Act of 1936, for example, infringed the principle about as
thoroughly as had the Federal Water Power Act of 1920. And
the Army Engineers' design of many pork barrel projects before and after the New Deal testified to the frailty of the progressive conservationists' dream.

But TVA's own performance won the respect even of some
of its critics. Arthur Morgan's key decision to use the Authority's own employees in construction, instead of contracting it
out to private firms as the government usually did, enabled
TVA to assemble an exceptionally competent staff of engineers and builders. TVA's dams practically always ran ahead
of schedule, a record unheard of in the private construction
industry. Its labor relations were almost unbelievably good,
in an era of union violence and sit-down strikes. From the
beginning TVA recognized its employees' right to bargain
collectively, and the mechanisms of labor-management consultation developed by the Authority and the unions seldom
failed to achieve peace and amicability. The work itself at-

tained a uniformly high quality. "Here," said Lewis Mumford of TVA's dams, "is modern architecture at its mightiest and its best."[7]

Few of the many journalists who visited the Valley failed to comment on the efficiency and public spirit of the Authority's employees, who numbered about 16,000 by 1935. The subsequent careers of TVA alumni suggested either that the board members and their personnel officers had chosen exceptional men in the first place, or that the men selected benefited marvelously from their TVA experience. Perhaps they demonstrated both. Henry Fowler, a young TVA lawyer in the 1930s, became in the 1960s President Johnson's secretary of the treasury. Julius Krug, one of the negotiators of the TEPCO sale, succeeded Harold Ickes as secretary of the interior under President Truman. Joseph Swidler, the other TEPCO negotiator, became TVA's general counsel, then Chairman of both the Federal Power Commission and the New York Public Service Commission. Two career employees, Gordon Clapp and Aubrey Wagner, ascended the administrative ladder to the TVA chairmanship. John D. Williams, who headed the experimental school system in Norris, was later chancellor of the University of Mississippi. John B. Blandford, the Authority's first general manager, served as assistant director of the Budget and administrator of the National Housing Agency. James Lawrence Fly became chairman of the Federal Communications Commission. J. Haden Alldredge, a TVA economist, became chairman of the Interstate Commerce Commission.

Its excellent personnel, the soundness of its administrative methods, the splendid construction work, and the physical and psychological benefits it brought to the Valley won the Authority a very high reputation. Even Wendell Willkie conceded that the TVA, regardless of the philosophy behind it, was an outstanding organization. And those observers inclined to favor the New Deal singled out TVA for special, and sometimes excessive praise. The historian Henry Steele Commager, for example, ignoring social security, economic growth, and the labor movement, pronounced TVA "probably the greatest peacetime achievement of twentieth-century America."[8]

This high reputation, though on the whole well-deserved, did not just emerge spontaneously. TVA pushed it along in a variety of ways, much as the private tradition had done for itself in the 1920s. The Authority's Information Office was one of its best units. Headed by William L. Sturdevant, a shrewd veteran of several Scripps-Howard editorships, the Information Office included among its dozen staff members a director of motion pictures as well as writers specializing in power, agriculture, and engineering. Sturdevant had the full support of the board of directors, who invited him to their own meetings beginning in 1935. Lilienthal in particular acutely appreciated TVA's need for good political and public relations. He selected as his two principal assistants a former administrative aide to one of the United States senators from Tennessee, and a former newspaperman with valuable press contacts.

TVA broadcast its story in many ways. Formal press releases, issued freely at first, gradually diminished in number to those containing real news and certain to be published. The Authority encouraged its employees to publish pieces in trade journals, and they responded with a deluge of articles (most of them cleared beforehand by the Information Office), in agricultural, legal, engineering, and economic publications. Lilienthal and Arthur Morgan each submitted numerous articles to trade and mass-circulation magazines, and made scores of speeches before a variety of local and national audiences. TVA's staff sent personal replies to each of the one hundred thousand letters of inquiry received from 1933 to 1940.[9]

The Information Office prepared and widely distributed fifteen major pamphlets, most of them written by professionals and liberally illustrated with photographs. *The Nation* judged one TVA pamphlet, entitled "Soil—the Nation's Basic Heritage," one of the 100 best publications of the year. Classes at Harvard, Yale, Columbia, and Princeton used the "Soil" pamphlet, as did Valley high schools and farmers' groups. The mailing list for TVA publications included (at the recipients' request), 185 Congressmen, 2000 libraries, 122 national and 156 Valley newspapers, 93 Washington correspondents, and 47 magazines.

TVA's photographers produced a striking visual record of the Authority's work, and received several national awards. Eastman Kodak used their pictures in some of its own exhibits. *The Architectural Forum* published a special TVA issue, noting that the accompanying portfolio contained "the most superb photographs the *Forum* has been privileged to present." The *New York Times* selected a TVA print for its list of outstanding pictures of the decade. In 1941 the Museum of Modern Art in New York held a one-agency show of TVA photographs and exhibits which subsequently went on a nationwide tour.[10]

The Authority set up exhibits at hundreds of professional conventions and meetings, and at schools and colleges throughout the country. It sent display teams to the Great Lakes Exposition in Cleveland, the Texas Centennial Exposition in Dallas, the International Exposition in Paris, the Golden Gate International Exposition in San Francisco, and the Museum of Science and Industry in New York. About 3.3 million persons saw the TVA exhibit at New York's World's Fair of 1939.

In TVA's first seven years, an estimated 4.3 million persons visited the rising dams, where they were met by trained guides equipped with information about the entire program. The plaque riveted conspicuously onto all TVA projects, with its legend "Built for the People of the United States," could tingle the spine of even a dubious visitor. For those who could not come, TVA prepared motion pictures. Hundreds of schools used these films, and by 1940 almost one million viewers, not counting the even larger number who saw them at expositions, had seen such movies as *TVA at Work, Norris Dam,* and *Electricity on the Farm.*

The TVA Technical Library prepared cumulative bibliographies with semiannual supplements which it mailed to 500 large libraries across the country. By 1936 TVA's researchers had counted more than a thousand magazine articles devoted to the Authority, and by 1940 more than two thousand. Some were hostile comments from utility spokesmen or other critics, but most were favorable. TVA itself provided photographs for illustrating a large number of these articles.[11]

To keep itself well informed, the Authority subscribed to an average of almost 500 periodicals and more than 100 newspapers. The Technical Library prepared a daily clipping service and news digest for circulation within the management staff. TVA aggressively promoted sympathy for the project among its own employees, offering them a course in "The Meaning of TVA."

Visting writers received special treatment. Trained members of the information staff guided them to construction sites and gave every possible assistance in researching their articles. TVA ordered reprints of especially favorable pieces and used them "to replace self-glorifying statements concerning the Authority by the Authority." Such writers as R.L. Duffus, Jonathan Daniels, and John Franklin Carter were among the many journalists judged "especially worthy of attention." Their laudatory treatments of TVA were priceless assets to the public relations campaign. With deliberate self-interest the Technical Library also went out of its way to assist graduate students investigating the program. "It might be expected that most of these students will be teachers," noted Sturdevant. "After a year's study of TVA, it would be impossible for them to be anything but sympathetic about the TVA program."[12]

Thus the Authority engaged in some of the kinds of public relations for which Norris, Roosevelt, and others had earlier condemned the private tradition. Most of TVA's publicity offended nobody, focusing as it did on the superb program of

unified river development and the goal of "electricity for all."
But some of it also contained political material, such as denun-
ciations of holding companies and unweighted comparisons
of TVA's electric rates with those of private companies. As
this propaganda became an issue in constitutional litigation,
TVA had trouble explaining it to the courts, and its publicists
grew more careful about what they said and wrote.

TVA easily won the fight for the loyalty of the Tennessee
Valley. Nationally too the Authority had some advantages.
The project itself, a new kind of public undertaking, was ir-
resistibly interesting. President Roosevelt's continuing love
affair with TVA and frequent public praise of it provided an
asset the private tradition could not match. One journalist,
after talking with Roosevelt in 1936, wrote that the Tennessee
Valley Authority was "the apple of his eye."[13]

Yet the private tradition had assets too. Where the Authority was regional, the private tradition was a formidable national presence embodied in hundreds of local companies.
These companies in turn represented hundreds of thousands
of individual and institutional investors who had a direct
pecuniary interest in confining public power to the New
Deal's scattered experiments and the existing municipal public plants. Furthermore, the private tradition had natural allies, comprising practically the entire business community.
The spokesmen of this huge group, such as the United States
Chamber of Commerce and the National Association of Manufacturers, regularly denounced TVA.

One of the most active of the utilities' allies was the coal industry. The National Coal Association, fearing injury from
TVA's hydro program, distributed thousands of copies of pamphlets attacking the "rubber yardstick" and quoting from Judge
Grubb's decision against TVA in the Ashwander case. Coal
companies in Alabama sent out copies of Wendell Willkie's
speeches, as well as their own leaflets attacking the Authority. Appalachian Coals, Incorporated, published a pamphlet

alleging that hydro power cost much more than coal-fired steam power. "TVA," said the company, meant "The Vision Asinine."[14]

During the presidential campaign of 1936, the Republican National Committee issued a somewhat fatuous press release purporting to link Arthur Morgan with the Soviet Union. Morgan had favored diplomatic recognition of the USSR and had served "on the advisory committee of the 'Open Road,' an affiliate with Intourist, Soviet-owned tourist agency." In 1935 the American Liberty League denounced the TVA amendments in a well-written pamphlet charging that the legislation attempted "to legalize some of these unlawful acts and to bestow even greater powers upon a bureaucratic menace."[15]

These efforts helped, but the utilities themselves propagandized best. The Alabama Power Company in particular filled the pages of state newspapers with slickly written (and sometimes untruthful) advertisements warning its customers to stick with established private companies. These ads alleged that TVA's customers had no appeal from disputes with the "unregulated" Authority and that the organizers of rural co-ops might be personally liable for their organizations' losses. Commonwealth and Southern took out ads in areas where neither its own subsidiaries nor TVA operated. "There is no question," an Ohio engineer wrote Lilienthal concerning an advertisement in the Toledo *Blade*, "but that Mr. Wilkie's [sic] cleverly prepared propaganda is quite effective, particularly inasmuch as it is read by a great number of people who are not at all conversant with the facts of the case."[16]

"I want to say," Willkie declared early in 1935, "that as propaganda artists we have come to learn that we were the most immature and bungling amateurs," in comparison with the federal government.[17] Actually nobody better illustrated the error of the statement than Willkie himself. From 1933 until well past his presidential campaign in 1940, he criticized the TVA and the New Deal power program more persistently and effectively than anyone else. His arguments seldom varied during this period, but his tone grew increasingly bitter and emotional. As he assumed the leadership of the entire business community late in the decade, Willkie's attack branched out, and he talked less of the TVA, more of private enterprise and federal encroachment. He almost always gave a virtuoso performance, whether his audience was other businessmen, congressional committees, or readers of the many periodicals in which he published articles.[18] He outdebated the New Deal's Robert Jackson in one noteworthy appearance, and made a superb impression on the "Information Please" radio program.

One Willkie theme hit TVA in its most vulnerable spot: "Whenever a householder in Tupelo, Mississippi, switches on a light, everybody in the United States helps to pay for it." TVA did help its own section, but at the expense of the whole country, "a fact which has given rise to the very pertinent remark that the Tennessee River touches five states and drains the nation." The administration's campaign against the utilities "is merely a prelude to similar action concerning other industries," which had better join the fight against the New Deal at once. Willkie usually avoided the redbaiting characteristic of much TVA criticism, but could still observe that some of the Authority's supporters were among "those who since the great war have become enamored with European economic and social concepts, and seek their application to American life." Most of all, Willkie charged that the New Deal had failed to bring recovery, and instead had created a crisis in business confidence that made normal cyclical recovery impossible. "Public abuse and punishment have failed to produce reemployment and economic rehabilitation," he insisted. And he asked with passion, " ... Is it not wise to seek to recover the good things we had in the days of our prosperity under a system of free enterprise and cooperation?" Much of Willkie's argument was undiluted Babbittry, but sometimes he made good sense. He effectively portrayed himself as the New Deal's chief individual victim, and had some sucess in fitting the private tradition into the mainstream of American history.

When the Supreme Court's turnabout of 1937 began to produce decisions upholding the New Deal, many businessmen shifted their first line of defense from their attorneys to their public relations men. The American "way of life" increasingly keynoted corporate advertising.[19] Willkie himself made a similar shift, fitting the role of salesman of private enterprise as comfortably as he had that of litigious challenger of the TVA and the Holding Company Act. "When businessmen commiserate with me," he wrote after the TEPCO sale, "because Government competition has cost us one of our companies, I am inclined to warn them, very frankly, that they may be next on the list. Their protection lies now, not in the courts but in the people."

Willkie frequently complained that Roosevelt's power program upset the market for utility securities and therefore retarded investment and recovery. About two hundred thousand investors owned C & S stocks and bonds, and a far larger number owned securities of other holding companies or operating companies. Together these investors formed an enormous constituency which transcended party lines and lent a ready ear to Willkie's rhetoric. They mailed thousands of letters to congressmen and federal bureaucrats. "Socking millionaires is fine business politically," a Commonwealth and Southern shareholder wrote Lilienthal, "but what about the little yaps like myself?" Another investor appealed to Louis Howe: "May I suggest that this part of the New Deal, be reshuffled, for another deal."[20]

The point was more than academic, and applied to more than the hardships of individuals. Market uncertainty, said Willkie and other utility men, deprived the economy of several billion dollars in electric plant expansion that would accelerate national recovery far better than the New Deal's pump-priming. Widely current throughout the thirties, the "investment destruction" argument hit with special force during the recession of 1937–1938.

Business confidence is no figment of the imagination, but it is intangible and incapable of direct measurement. Like most other securities, utility stocks had dropped sharply long before Roosevelt's inauguration. Yet no one could deny that his policies affected the market. His announcement of the power pool conference boosted the exchange price of C & S common. The January 4 contract, which limited TVA's territory, caused a jump in price of Alabama Power's preferred stock. And a New York brokerage house calculated that utility securities as a whole experienced "a drastic and unprecedented depreciation" totalling almost a billion dollars during seven weeks in the fall of 1934. During this period the Baker-Beck opinion, Roosevelt's Tupelo speech, and especially the emerging holding company legislation suggested that the New Deal and the utilities were about to begin a death struggle.[21]

Yet the constant flow of gloomy pronouncements from Willkie and other executives hardly enhanced the appeal of their securities. The predictions of impending doom had elements of self-fulfilling prophecy. "After all," said a reply TVA drafted for the White House to send to a complaining investor, "if the management of a company persistently asserts that ruin stares it in the face, can any investor be expected to think highly of its securities?" And the Federal Trade Commission's disclosures of frenzied finance in the power business may have had more to do with the market decline than did all of Roosevelt's power programs.[22]

Some government spokesmen considered the companies' behavior to be pure spite, amounting to a deliberate strike of capital. "It is my belief," Chairman Frank McNinch of the Federal Power Commission wrote Roosevelt, "that the failure of the utilities to undertake this construction has been prompted by political strategy rather than business principles." Whatever the cause, the effect was clear. Private com-

panies' construction during the thirties lagged badly, amounting to only about two-fifths, and in some years much less, the
rate for 1925–1930. Harping constantly on the investment destruction theme, utility spokesmen laid the blame at the door
of the New Deal. A TVA employee counted over sixty ex-
pressions of this argument in the press during the eighteen
months beginning in October 1937. That the point conflicted
with the frequent assertion from the same sources that there
was no shortage of power, and hence no need for federal hydro
projects, seemed not to reduce its effectiveness. The public
wanted recovery, and the New Deal had not provided it. The
return of severe economic depression in 1937, Lilienthal told
Norris, gave the point special credence. "The argument is
specious and in some respects brazen, but I think we ought to
be honest with ourselves and admit that it is making a con-
siderable impression on public opinion."[23]

Utility men also complained that TVA and PWA hampered
the refinancing of bond issues. Taking advantage of the depression's low-cost money market, Willkie pushed through for
his northern companies a refunding program that cut their
capital costs and permitted rate reductions. A similar operation for the southern group could not take place, he often said,
because of the TVA.

Facts supported this contention. As Preston Arkwright of
the Georgia Power Company wrote Roosevelt, removal of the
PWA-TVA threat would enable his company to "refund its
outstanding bonds on a 3½% basis where it now pays 5%, and
its Preferred stock on a 4½% basis where it now pays 6%."
Such an apparently small reduction would save the company
more than $2.5 million annually in fixed capital charges. This
figure, by comparison, amounted to a little over one-half of
Georgia Power's annual revenue from residential customers,
who could receive the benefit of rate reductions if refinancing
could go forward.[24] Unlike the "investment destruction" argument, the failure of the companies to refund their bonds almost certainly had no connection with political strategy. The

saving was too great to pass up, and the point itself too technical to be very useful in propaganda.

The strike of utility capital disturbed Roosevelt a great
deal. Looking for some compromise solution, he and his lieutenants held a series of private conferences with Willkie and
other executives, but the meetings accomplished little. Both
sides were distrustful and reluctant to yield. As war in Europe
began to appear likely in 1938, the issue grew urgent, and the
president appointed a National Defense Power Committee to
make plans for preventing the kind of national power shortage that had caught the country unprepared in 1917. Again
mutual suspicion prevented fruitful cooperation, and dissension within the government itself once more revealed
deep cleavages over administration policy. Militants wanted
to use national defense as a vehicle for advancing public
ownership. Moderates wanted better regulation of private
companies. Secretary Ickes wanted personal control of all
federal power operations. The private tradition clung to its
long discredited argument that there was no actual or potential shortage of electricity. Construction did increase markedly
at the turn of the decade, but not until the United States entered the war in 1941 and the full output of all public and
private plants became essential to national security was the
question settled.[25] The coming of the war forced an adjourn-
ment of the power fight.

The argument over war production which went on from
1938 until Pearl Harbor disclosed once again the separate
aims of different officials within the administration, and raised
anew the question of just what the New Deal's power policy
was. In retrospect, it is clear that no thoroughgoing and coherent policy existed. Jealous agencies shared a divided responsibility, and Roosevelt provided little specific guidance. Perhaps he wanted it that way. A keen student of the utility
question, he still lacked Morris Cooke's detailed vision of a
mixed national grid network, or George Norris's total devotion

to public power, or David Lilienthal's transcendent faith in the valley authority idea. Probably — and this was true of many other economic problems as well — Roosevelt never thought the issue through to a satisfactory conclusion. Instead he preferred to deal with immediate questions separately as they arose.

By 1940 FDR had achieved many of his goals, had failed to achieve others, and had not even attempted what many public power advocates and most of the private tradition half-expected him to attempt. REA showed that rural electrification could pay its way with only a little assistance from the government. TVA demonstrated dramatically that low rates brought increased consumption; and, together with the breathtaking Bonneville and Grand Coulee projects of the Pacific Northwest, stood as a splendid example of regional public power. The New Deal undoubtedly brought holding companies under control. Even as progressive a company as Commonwealth and Southern had to split into northern and southern groups (in 1947, following prolonged negotiations with the Securities and Exchange Commission). All holding companies had to submit their financial transactions to close government scrutiny, and most underwent rigorous writedowns of their capitalization. Roosevelt created a national awareness of the obligations of public utilities, and helped identify the best and the worst companies, even if he treated them with equal contempt.

The New Deal did not convert the private tradition to a full acceptance of the public utility idea. It failed to insure the effectiveness of existing state regulatory machinery — a question mostly beyond federal remedy. And it failed to present a united, coherent policy so that the public, the industry, and government officials themselves could know exactly what to expect. Roosevelt achieved no structural alteration of the industry. He attempted none. He never seriously contemplated nationalization, and it is a nice question how far he could have gone if he had. Most of what he did accomplish came after the worst of the depression emergency apparently had passed, and the rough going of the holding company legislation of 1935 suggested the limits of what Congress and the public would accept. Essentially, Roosevelt rescued the industry from its own abuses, and thereby preserved it.

He might have done this much with a great deal less agitation and ill will. As John Maynard Keynes wrote him in 1938, the continuing attack on utilities "arises too much out of what is dead and gone. The real criminals have cleared out long ago," and the ongoing rhetoric benefited nobody. To Roosevelt Keynes laid down a specific challenge:

> Is it not for you to decide either to make real peace or to be much more drastic the other way? Personally I think there is a great deal to be said for the ownership of all the utilities by publicly owned boards. But if public opinion is not yet ripe for this, what is the object of chasing the utilities round the lot every other week?[26]

One might infer from its title that the National Power Policy Committee unified the diverse aims present within the New Deal. But the committee's shilly-shallying in 1934 and 1935 presaged similar behavior later. When Roosevelt reconstituted the group in 1937 to deal with the problem of disposing of power from the Bonneville project, some members, such as Morris L. Cooke and John Carmody, wanted also to formulate a broad national power policy. Others wanted to hold public hearings on Bonneville. But as Benjamin Cohen pointed out, "If we have public hearings, I am wondering if the expression of the different views of the people in the government may not prove to be embarrassing." So the committee met in private, and concerned itself with the immediate problem only.[27] In the third life of the NPPC, into which the National Defense Power Committee merged as part of an attempted personal coup by Ickes, the immediate problem was war production, and the question of broad policy again failed to appear on the agenda.

Nothing better illustrated the government's fragmentation than the effort in 1937 and 1938 to proliferate valley authorities. When Roosevelt recommended TVA legislation in 1933 he said "If we are successful here we can march on, step by step, in a like development of other great natural territorial units within our borders." Implicit in Norris's thought from the beginning was the idea that a successful TVA would spawn valley authorities everywhere. Early in 1937, Norris suggested the establishment of "enough TVA's to cover the entire country," and introduced appropriate legislation.[28] His proposal encountered immediate and violent opposition not only from the private tradition but from Secretary of Agriculture Wallace and Secretary of War Woodring, both of whom protested that valley authorities would duplicate their departments' work. And even those who wanted regional authorities, such as Ickes and Lilienthal, disagreed among themselves over whether the new agencies would be independent, like TVA, or under the jurisdiction of the Department of Interior. Ickes never relented in his effort to crown himself the administration's power czar, and Lilienthal and Norris never stopped trying to keep TVA independent.[29] The constant reiteration of the Authority's rhetoric about grass roots democracy and administrative decentralization during the period when Ickes was trying to take over the TVA suggests that the arguments themselves developed by way of self defense.

Despite his personal enchantment with the TVA, Roosevelt persistently equivocated on the valley authority idea. He blew hot and cold on Ickes's appeals for personal control. He refused to give clear support for either Norris's "seven sisters" proposal or for its competition, a bill which would set up conservation authorities with planning functions but without the funds and organization to execute their plans. The whole matter overlapped the complex question of conservation policy, and the dizzying issue of government reorganization. Valley authority legislation failed altogether in the late thirties (and later in the mid-forties, when Congressman Rankin brought it up again), for many of the same reasons that reorganization failed—hostility and dissension within the government and opposition from private interests which believed themselves threatened.

In retrospect, the real wonder is that a single TVA ever materialized. The reasons that it did lie in the history of American crisis politics during the twentieth century. The crisis of 1917 produced Wilson Dam. The depression dramatized the urgency for reform of the power industry, and simultaneously created a need for economic relief and public works. The succeeding emergency, World War II, occasioned a huge growth of TVA's power production. Brought into being by the stimulus of the depression, the Authority as a going concern proved adaptable to national demands beyond those of the New Deal. As Jonathan Daniels wrote Roosevelt in 1944, "TVA seems to me the best and most understandable symbol in the South and out of it of the present demonstration of the practical good sense of the New Deal. Its war record provides the best connecting link between the New Deal and your present Win-the-War position." TVA electricity in great quantities went into the manufacture of aluminum for warplanes. And after 1945, continuing crises promoted still further growth. The Korean and Cold wars created a need, real or fancied, for large stockpiles of fissionable materials. Uranium reduction required vast amounts of power, and at one point during the 1950s more than one-half of TVA's enormous production went to the Atomic Energy Commission's plants at Oak Ridge and Paducah. "More than is commonly realized," wrote the political scientist Aaron Wildavsky, "the growth of TVA has been a product of war."[30]

During the few years of relative calm after 1945, TVA's appropriations dropped sharply, reflecting the stinginess of the American Congress in nonmilitary spending. (The TVA Revenue Bond Act of 1959 finally solved the appropriations problem by making TVA self-financing.) Indeed, except during periods of emergency, the Authority has few political allies outside the Tennessee Valley, except in the public power states of the West. It has the relentless enmity of a strong interest group and the ideological opposition of every true believer in the purity of American free enterprise.

Critics of the TVA, like those of the New Deal in general, divide between those who oppose it on philosophical or self-interest grounds and those who believe it betrayed its opportunity as an economic planner. By their own standards, both sets of critics are correct. TVA is "socialistic," because the public owns the means of its power production. And TVA is not a regional planner in any thorough sense, although in the 1960s some of the ideas dormant since Arthur Morgan's dismissal experienced a revival whose outcome is not yet clear.

Both criticisms tend to obscure what TVA has actually done. The unified development of the Tennessee River was a spectacular achievement, unmatched for any other stream in the world. The Authority's power program is the largest and probably the most efficient in the United States. TVA has thus emerged as an authentic fulfillment of three principal ideas: the progressive conservationists' multiple-purpose approach to water resources, the public power tradition's promotion of high usage through low rates, and the American System's stimulation of the private marketplace through internal improvements. That the internal improvements include the anomaly of a socialistic power system is only because electricity is a vendible utility whose sale in TVA's case competed with established private interests. In the overall sense, even this advances the goal of promoting private economic activity with public assistance. Whether or not the money spent on TVA represents the optimum economic multiplier remains an unanswered question.[31]

When TVA designed its rate structure, increased use of electricity in homes seemed to be an unmitigated good. Yet, ever greater consumption of electricity now produces negative social effects as well as positive. Unlike hydroelectric dams, coal and nuclear fired steam plants pollute the environment, in almost every conceivable way. Strip mining of coal ravages the countryside. Burning coal pollutes the air. Nuclear power presents a constant problem of waste disposal and danger of accident. Both coal and nuclear plants heat huge quantities of water, killing aquatic organisms and upsetting the ecological balance.

But these questions face another generation. The men who went to the Tennessee Valley in 1933, or already lived there, faced a different set of questions. They developed a set of answers, and defended them in a battle between government and business as intense as any in American history. "When I think of the work which has been done," George Norris reflected in 1941, "and the difficulties which have beset those in charge of this project, and the malicious attempts made to destroy it by the power trust, I can hardly believe the development which has taken place." Now past eighty, Norris looked back with almost childlike wonder at the work to which he himself had made the largest contribution. "It seems, when I think it over, that it is too good to be true. It seems almost like a dream."[32]

NOTES

NOTE: Locations of cited manuscript collections and other unpublished sources are given on pages 191–192.

Preface, pp. vii-ix

[1] *Public Papers of the Presidents of the United States: John F. Kennedy, 1963* (Washington: Government Printing Office, 1964), p. 410; Eisenhower is quoted in Emmett John Hughes, *The Ordeal of Power: A Political Memoir of the Eisenhower Years* (New York: Atheneum, 1963), p. 152.

Chapter 1, pp. 1–25

[1] Lee DeForest, "Tomorrow, Who Knows?" *Saturday Evening Post,* CCII (August 10, 1929), 46, 51; F. R. Moulton, quoted in M. S. Sloan, "Electricity — Mankind's Universal Servant," *Annals* of the American Academy of Political and Social Science, CLIX (January, 1932), 140.

[2] Norris, *Fighting Liberal* (New York: Macmillan, 1945), p. 16. Unless otherwise noted this summary of Norris's life is from *Fighting Liberal* and from Richard Lowitt, *George W. Norris: The Making of a Progressive, 1861–1912* (Syracuse: Syracuse University Press, 1963).

[3] Norris, *Fighting Liberal,* pp. 92–93.

[4] *Ibid.,* pp. 160, 172, 248. See also

Alfred Lief, *Democracy's Norris: The Biography of a Lonely Crusade* (New York: Stackpole Sons, 1939), p. 257.

[5] Norris to George Fort Milton, February 7, 1926, Tray 69, box 8, Norris MSS.

[6] In what follows I have relied on Harold C. Passer, *The Electrical Manufacturers, 1870–1900: A Study in Competition, Entrepreneurship, Technical Change, and Economic Growth* (Cambridge: Harvard University Press, 1953); and Forrest McDonald's two books on the subject, *Let There Be Light: The Electric Utility Industry in Wisconsin, 1881–1955* (Madison: The American History Research Center, 1957), and *Insull* (Chicago: University of Chicago Press, 1962). See also Raymond C. Miller, *Kilowatts at Work: A History of the Detroit Edison Company* (Detroit: Wayne State University Press, 1957); Thomas W. Martin, *The Story of Electricity in Alabama since the Turn of the Century, 1900–1952* (Birmingham: The Company, 1952); and Wade H. Wright, *History of the Georgia Power Company 1855–1956* (Atlanta: Georgia Power Company, 1957).

⁷ The argument over rates, which symbolized the rivalry between the public and private traditions, was endless. Both sides, with periodic emissions of selected statistics, claimed victory. In general, the larger municipal plants had lower rates than most private companies, the smaller ones higher. This fact alone made the battle of statistics hopelessly confusing to the public. See William E. Mosher, ed., *Electrical Utilities: The Crisis in Public Control* (New York and London: Harper & Brothers, 1929), pp. 232–267, an important book because of its influence on Franklin D. Roosevelt.

The summary on utilities which follows can be found in slightly different forms in any textbook on utility economics, such as Eli W. Clemens, *Economics and Public Utilities* (New York: Appleton-Century-Crofts, 1950); Martin G. Glaeser, *Public Utilities in American Capitalism* (New York: Macmillan, 1957); Charles F. Phillips, Jr., *The Economics of Regulation: Theory and Practice in the Transportation and Public Utility Industries* (Homewood, Ill.: Richard D. Irwin, 1965); Paul J. Garfield and Wallace F. Lovejoy, *Public Utility Economics* (Englewood Cliffs, N. J.: Prentice-Hall, 1964). See also McDonald, *Let There Be Light*, pp. 93–96, 106–111.

⁸ This discussion of holding companies owes much to James C. Bonbright and Gardiner C. Means, *The Holding Company: Its Public Significance and its Regulation* (New York and London: McGraw-Hill, 1932); Norman S. Buchanan, "The Origin and Development of the Public Utility Holding Company," *Jour-*

nal of Political Economy, XLIV (February, 1936), 31-53; *Fortune*, "Commonwealth and Southern," XV (May, 1937), 83; and McDonald, *Let There Be Light*, pp. 186–201.

⁹ Clemens, *Economics and Public Utilities*, pp. 105, 461. See also Harold H. Young, *Forty Years of Public Utility Finance* (Charlottesville: University Press of Virginia, 1965), pp. 16–17.

¹⁰ M. H. Aylesworth, "National Electrical Development and Its Effect Upon Utility Regulation," NELA pamphlet, March, 1922.

¹¹ McDonald, *Insull*, p. 183 and *passim*.

¹² McDonald, *Insull, passim;* Samuel I. Rosenman, comp., *The Public Papers and Addresses of Franklin D. Roosevelt* (New York: Random House, 1938–1950; vols. 6–9 pub. by Macmillan, vols. 10–13 by Harper), I, 755.

¹³ 169 U. S. 466.

¹⁴ Norris to George Fort Milton, February 7, 1926, Tray 69, Box 8, Norris MSS.

¹⁵ *Ibid.;* Norris to Oliver Cunningham, December 29, 1930, Tray 66, box 6; to Edwin J. Clapp, March 28, 1928, Tray 67, box 7, p. 4; to Donald Richberg, October 14, 1931, Tray 26, box 4, all in Norris MSS.

¹⁶ Jerome G. Kerwin, *Federal Water-Power Legislation* (New York: Columbia University Press, 1926), pp. 65–66, 69–72, 73; Paul W. Gates and Robert W. Swenson, *History of Public Land Law Development* (Washington: Government Printing Office, 1968), pp. 659, 660, 685–692.

¹⁷ Pinchot, *The Fight for Conservation* (New York: Doubleday, Page,

1910), p. 54; Samuel P. Hays, *Conservation and the Gospel of Efficiency: The Progressive Conservation Movement, 1890–1920* (Cambridge: Harvard University Press, 1959), pp. 6–11, 114–121; Donald C. Swain, *Federal Conservation Policy, 1921–1933* (Berkeley and Los Angeles: University of California Press, 1963), Chapter VI; Johnny Booth Smallwood, "George W. Norris and the Concept of a Planned Region," unpublished doctoral dissertation, University of North Carolina, 1963, pp. 61–62, 76, 77; Richard Lowitt, "A Neglected Aspect of the Progressive Movement: George W. Norris and Public Control of Hydro-electric Power, 1913–1919," *Historian*, XXVII (May, 1965), 350-635.

[18] At Boulder Dam, finished in the thirties but planned in the twenties, the arrangement was that the government would build the dam but prospective customers, public and private, would provide the generating equipment, transmission lines, and their maintenance. The Los Angeles municipal plant acted for the public distributors, Southern California Edison for the private. This arrangement is a lucid reflection of the way the problem was viewed in the twenties, and stands in sharp contrast to public policy for the TVA and Bonneville projects of the thirties.

[19] *Fighting Liberal*, p. 251; William E. Leuchtenburg, *Flood Control Politics: The Connecticut River Valley Problem, 1927–1950* (Cambridge: Harvard University Press, 1953), p. 10.

[20] This summary of the Muscle Shoals question relies on Preston J. Hubbard, *Origins of the TVA: The Muscle Shoals Controversy, 1920–1932* (Nashville: Vanderbilt University Press, 1961), which traces the story with admirable clarity. See also C. Herman Pritchett, *The Tennessee Valley Authority: A Study in Public Administration* (Chapel Hill: University of North Carolina Press, 1943), Chapter 1; Sarah Elizabeth Bosely Winger, "The Genesis of TVA," unpublished doctoral dissertation, University of Wisconsin, 1959; and Frederic A. Benincasa, "An Analysis of the Historical Development of the Tennessee Valley Authority from 1933 to 1961," unpublished doctoral dissertation, St. John's University (New York), 1961, pp. 1–18.

[21] The first is by Carl D. Thompson (New York: E. P. Dutton, 1932); the second by H. S. Raushenbush (New York: New Republic, 1928); the third by Ernest Gruening (New York: Vanguard, 1931). The other three are M. L. Ramsay, *Pyramids of Power: The Story of Roosevelt, Insull and the Utility Wars* (New York and Indianapolis: Bobbs-Merrill, 1937); Jack Levin, *Power Ethics* (New York: Alfred A. Knopf, 1931); and Stephen Raushenbush, *The Power Fight* (New York: New Republic, 1932). These books vary widely in literary merit and reliability, the volumes by Gruening and Levin being the best of the lot on both counts.

[22] U. S., Federal Trade Commission, *Utility Corporations*, Senate Document 92, 70th Cong., 1st sess. (1934), 71A, pp. 14–16.

[23] Judson King, "Power Records of Hoover and Roosevelt: A Non-Partisan Analysis for the Information

of Voters," National Popular Government League Bulletin 157, September 9, 1932, pp. 8–9; Hoover Address to NELA (also broadcast over the radio), May 21, 1924, excerpts in Tray 26, box 4, Norris MSS; Leuchtenburg, *Flood Control Politics*, p. 11.

[24] *Utility Corporations*, 71A, 18; Alan R. Raucher, *Public Relations and Business, 1900–1929* (Baltimore: Johns Hopkins Press, 1963), p. 91.

[25] *New York Times*, January 14, 15, 1933; Edison Electric Institute *Bulletin*, I (December 1933), 282, 284.

[26] Hubbard, *Origins of the TVA*, p. 177 and Chapter IX.

[27] U. S., President, *Veto Message Relating to Disposition of Muscle Shoals*, Senate Document 321, 71st Cong., 3rd sess. (1931), pp. 1–3.

Notes for Chapter 2, pp. 26–46

[1] The best accounts of FDR's gubernatorial experience with the power issue are Bernard Bellush, *Franklin D. Roosevelt as Governor of New York* (New York: Columbia University Press, 1955), pp. 208–268; and Frank Freidel, *Franklin D. Roosevelt: The Triumph* (Boston: Little, Brown, 1956), pp. 43–46, 81–83, 100–119. Unless otherwise noted this summary is from these two sources.

[2] Daniel R. Fusfeld, *The Economic Thought of Franklin D. Roosevelt and the Origins of the New Deal* (New York and London: Columbia University Press, 1956), pp. 27–30, 35–36.

[3] Freidel, *The Triumph*, pp. 118–119. See also Roosevelt, *Public Papers and Addresses*, I, 420–421.

[4] Quoted in Arthur M. Schlesinger,

Jr., *The Crisis of the Old Order 1919–1933* (Boston: Houghton Mifflin, 1957), p. 70.

[5] Quoted in Fusfeld, *The Economic Thought of Franklin D. Roosevelt*, p. 144. See also Freidel, *The Triumph*, p. 100; Franklin D. Roosevelt, "The Real Meaning of the Power Problem," *Forum*, LXXXII (December, 1929), 327–330; Roosevelt, *Government—Not Politics* (New York: Covici, Friede, 1932), pp. 45–47; and Roosevelt, *Public Papers and Addresses*, I, 728–729.

[6] David E. Lilienthal, unpublished journal, entry of May 14, 1935, Lilienthal MSS.

[7] Fusfeld, *The Economic Thought of Franklin D. Roosevelt*, pp. 59–62, 253, 270 n15, 284–285 n35; Freidel, *Franklin D. Roosevelt: The Apprenticeship* (Boston: Little, Brown, 1952), p. 210. The Navy built a plant, but it was decommissioned by the Harding administration in 1920.

[8] Cooke to Norris, June 23, 1932; King to Norris, September 13, 1932, p. 3, both in Tray 1, box 4, Norris MSS; Moley, *After Seven Years* (New York and London: Harper & Brothers, 1939), p. 12. See Also Freidel, *The Triumph*: "There was no other area, even that of agriculture, in which Roosevelt undertook such intensive study." (p. 101.)

[9] His consultation with Frankfurter can be traced in Max Freedman, annotator, *Roosevelt and Frankfurter: Their Correspondence 1928–1945* (Boston and Toronto: Little, Brown, 1967), pp. 35, 41, 43–45, 54–57.

[10] Norris to Basil Manly, September 1, 1932; King to Norris, September 13, 1932, both in Tray 1, box 4,

Norris MSS; the King pamphlet is Bulletin 157 of the National Popular Government League, dated September 9, 1932.

[11] Roosevelt, *Public Papers and Addresses*, I, 738–739.

[12] *Ibid.*, pp. 733, 736, 737, 740, 742.

[13] Freidel, *The Triumph*, p. 353; Lief, *Democracy's Norris*, p. 403.

[14] Lief, *Democracy's Norris*, p. 406; Schlesinger, *The Coming of the New Deal* (Boston: Houghton Mifflin, 1958), p. 324.

[15] Roosevelt, *Public Papers and Addresses*, I, 888–889; II, 122.

[16] The sections are 22 and 23 of the Tennessee Valley Authority Act of May 18, 1933 (48 Stat. 58); interview with Morgan, March 29, 1967.

[17] U. S., House, Committee on Military Affairs, *Muscle Shoals*, 73rd Cong., 1st sess. (1933), pp. 115, 159, 169, 223, 225. The fullest description of the final battle over transmission lines is in Judson King, *The Conservation Fight: From Theodore Roosevelt to the Tennessee Valley Authority* (Washington: Public Affairs Press, 1959), pp. 271–276.

[18] Much of what follows in the remainder of this chapter is a condensation of Chapter II of Thomas K. McCraw, *Morgan vs. Lilienthal: The Feud Within the TVA* (Chicago: Loyola University Press, 1970).

[19] Morgan, "Transforming the American College System," *Current History*, XXXII (July, 1930), 719.

[20] Quoted in Webb Waldron, "Boss of Muscle Shoals," *American Magazine*, CXVI (August, 1933), 125.

[21] 48 Stat. 59.

[22] Harcourt Morgan, preface to a projected but uncompleted book, n.d. (c. 1950), p. 1, Harcourt Morgan MSS.

[23] Interviews with Neil Bass (former assistant of H. A. Morgan), June 12, 1967; with Dr. Lucy and Miss Fay Morgan (daughters of H. A. Morgan), June 16, 1967; Harcourt Morgan, transcript of recorded interview, n.d. (c. 1949), spool 3, p. 3, Harcourt Morgan MSS.

[24] Arthur Morgan to Marvin McIntyre, telegram, May 29, 1933, Arthur Morgan MSS.

[25] Harcourt Morgan, address to regional meeting of the NELA, n.d. (1927), Memphis, Tennessee, copy in TVA Technical Library, Knoxville, Tennessee.

[26] Arthur Morgan, "A Statement of My Relations with the President," unpublished memorandum, two parts, July 1 and 5, 1938, I, 8, Arthur Morgan MSS.

[27] Norris to Morris L. Cooke, July 8, 1933; Norris to Lewis C. Gray, Ernest Gruening, Cooke, others (telegrams), June 6 and 7, 1933, all in Norris MSS; King to Cooke, May 31, 1933, King MSS; King, "Keep Your Eye on the Ball," National Popular Government League Bulletin 183, March 17, 1938.

[28] Lilienthal to Felix Frankfurter, June 6, 1924, Lilienthal MSS.

[29] Frankfurter to Lilienthal, June 4, 1924, Lilienthal MSS.

[30] Lilienthal, "Utility Rates in the Depression," address to the League of Wisconsin Municipalities, June 22, 1932, at Menasha, Wisconsin, p. 13; Lilienthal, "Current Issues in Public Utility Regulation," address to the League of Women Voters, March 11, 1933, at Chicago, p. 4;

Lilienthal, "Government and the Public Utilities," address under the auspices of the Institute of Economics, Jan 24, 1933, at Washington, D. C., p. 1, all in files of the Wisconsin Public Service Commission, Madison.

[31] Eli W. Clemens, "Public Utility Regulation in Wisconsin since the Reorganization of the Commission in 1931," unpublished doctoral dissertation, University of Wisconsin, 1940, p. 11.

[32] Lilienthal, unpublished journal, Nov. 5, 1932; the date of the conversation with Maltbie is recorded as Oct. 13, 1932, Lilienthal MSS. A copy of the draft legislation is in box 66 of the Felix Frankfurter MSS; Edward Meeman to Lowell Mellett, May 27, 1933, copy in George Fort Milton MSS.

[33] Freedman, annotator, *Roosevelt and Frankfurter*, p. 138. The date of Frankfurter's letter was June 6, 1933.

[34] Norris to Allen J. Roulhac, June 16, 1933, Tray 81, box 7, Norris MSS.

Notes for Chapter 3, pp. 47–66

[1] Harcourt Morgan, "TVA Connection," part of a projected but unfinished book, n.d. (c. 1950), p. 2, Harcourt Morgan MSS; Minutes of the Board Meetings, TVA Records, Knoxville, meeting of June 16, 1933 (hereafter cited as Board Minutes).

[2] Willkie to Morgan, June 13, 1933, in Administrative Files, TVA Archives, Knoxville (hereafter cited as TVA Archives); Board Minutes, June 16, 1933.

[3] Unless otherwise noted the summary which follows is from Ellsworth Barnard, *Wendell Willkie . . . Fighter for Freedom* (Marquette: Northern Michigan University Press, 1966), Chapters 1–5; and Joseph Barnes, *Willkie: The Events He Was Part of — the Ideas He Fought for* (New York: Simon and Schuster, 1952), Chapters 1–4. Two other biographies are Mary E. Dillon, *Wendell Willkie, 1892–1944* (Philadelphia: J. B. Lippincott, 1952); and Alden Hatch, *Young Willkie* (New York: Harcourt, Brace, 1944).

[4] See, for example, the synthesis of press comments in Maxine Block, ed., *Current Biography 1940* (New York: H. W. Wilson, 1940), p. 876.

[5] Quoted in Barnard, *Wendell Willkie*, p. 57.

[6] Quoted in Barnes, *Willkie*, p. 35.

[7] Bonbright and Means, *The Holding Company*, pp. 185–186.

[8] FTC, *Utility Corporations*, Vol. 78, 1–16; Barnes, *Willkie*, pp. 49–51; Barnard, *Wendell Willkie*, pp. 80–81; "Commonwealth & Southern," *Fortune*, XV (May, 1937), 83–86.

[9] "Make no mistake about it," David Lilienthal said in 1967, "he was put in there to deal with TVA." (Interview with Lilienthal, June 4, 1967.) Willkie was the hand-picked successor to the ailing Bernard C. Cobb, who wrote Roosevelt in 1933 that his stockholders were "vitally concerned with respect to whether the Federal Government shall engage in the business of transmitting and distributing electricity in competition with them." Cobb to Roosevelt, January 30, 1933; see also Cobb to Roosevelt, February 28, April 7 and 8, 1933; C. A. Beasley, memorandum for Marvin McIntyre (FDR's

secretary), April 3, 1933; Beasley, memorandum for Stephen Early (another secretary), March 10, 1933, all in Official Files (cited hereafter as OF) 42 and 44, Roosevelt MSS.

[10] Murray Friedman, "Voyage of a Liberal: Wendell L. Willkie," unpublished doctoral dissertation, Georgetown University, 1958, pp. 53–54.

[11] 48 Stat. 58, Sections 9(a), 10, 11, 12, 12(a), 14, and 22.

[12] The Act did stipulate that if TVA contracted to sell power which would be resold at a profit, the contract was cancellable on five years' notice, at the end of which the private companies must relinquish their claim to a preference customer.

[13] Arthur Morgan, memorandum of meeting, June 28, 1933, Arthur Morgan MSS.

[14] McCraw, *Morgan vs. Lilienthal*, pp. 31–33.

[15] Arthur Morgan, "Suggested Introduction to Statement on Power Policy," memorandum, July 1938, pp. 5–6; Arthur Morgan to Harcourt Morgan and Lilienthal, memorandum on power policy, August 14, 1933, pp. 1–6, Arthur Morgan MSS.

[16] Lilienthal, "Memorandum in Opposition to Proposal of Chairman A. E. Morgan for Territorial Division Agreement and 'Cooperation' between Tennessee Valley Authority and Private Utilities," August 16, 1933, Arthur Morgan MSS; Lilienthal to Felix Frankfurter, note attached to Morgan memorandum of August 14, 1933, Box 71, Frankfurter MSS.

[17] Lilienthal to Morgan, July 21, 1933 (photostat); Lilienthal, "Memorandum in Opposition to Proposal

of Chairman A. E. Morgan . . . ," August 16, 1933, Arthur Morgan MSS; Board Minutes, July 11, 1933.

[18] Arthur Morgan to Lilienthal and Harcourt Morgan, August 14, 1933, pp. 5–6, Arthur Morgan MSS; Lilienthal to Norris, August 17, 1933, Tray 69, box 4, Norris MSS.

[19] The release is printed in full in TVA's first *Annual Report*, pp. 22–24; a copy of Lilienthal's first draft is in Tray 69, box 4, Norris MSS. See also U.S., Congress, *Hearings* Before the Joint Committee on the Investigation of the Tennessee Valley Authority, 75th Cong., 3rd sess. (Washington: Government Printing Office, 1939), pp. 772–773, 785–786; hereafter cited as *Hearings*.

[20] Willkie emphasized the positive: "I shall be very glad to discuss the cooperative features [of the power policy] with you and Mr. Lilienthal, or either of you." Willkie to Arthur Morgan, August 30, 1933, TVA Archives.

[21] Swidler, interview in Memphis State University Oral History Project (1969). The discussion which follows is based on *Hearings*, pp. 753–807, 5309, 5314–5315, 5615–5617; *Engineering Report* of the Joint Committee Investigating the Tennessee Valley Authority (Senate Document 56, 76th Cong., 1st sess., Part 3), Section 9; Clemens, *Economics and Public Utilities*, pp. 622–624; Glaeser, *Public Utilities in American Capitalism*, pp. 556–567; contemporary working papers of the consultants in the Martin G. Glaeser MSS; and Richard L. Wallace, "TVA's Pricing of Electric Power," unpublished doctoral dissertation, Vanderbilt University, 1965, *passim*.

[22] At various times the consultants included Walter Polakov, an engineer and author; Professor Martin G. Glaeser of the University of Wisconsin; E. W. Morehouse and Haninah Zinder of the Wisconsin Public Service Commission; James C. Bonbright and Leland Olds of the New York Power Authority; and Milo R. Maltbie of the New York Public Service Commission. TVA's chief rate expert was Edward Falck, a bright young utility economist.

[23] *Hearings*, p. 5314.

[24] TVA press release, September 14, 1933, TVA Technical Library, Knoxville; *Hearings*, p. 5315; B. C. Cobb to Roosevelt, April 7, 1933, p. 2, gives slightly different figures for the companies (OF 44, Roosevelt MSS).

[25] TVA press release, September 15, 1933, TVA Technical Library, Knoxville.

[26] Lilienthal to Marvin McIntyre, November 21, 1933, with attached memorandum, OF 42, Roosevelt MSS. On the consumer-credit aspect of the plan, see Joseph D. Coppock, "Government as Enterpriser-Competitor: The Case of the Electric Home and Farm Authority," *Explorations in Entrepreneurial History*, I (Winter, 1964), 187–206.

[27] Lilienthal, "Memorandum in Opposition to Proposal of Chairman A. E. Morgan...," August 16, 1933, Arthur Morgan MSS; Arthur Morgan to Willkie, September 2, 1933; Lilienthal to Willkie, September 6, 1933; Willkie to Lilienthal, September 11, 1933, all in TVA Archives; Lilienthal, *The TVA Years 1939–1945* (New York: Harper and Row, 1964), p. 711.

[28] Lilienthal to the board, memorandum, "Basis for Negotiation," October 13, 1933, p. 8, TVA Archives.

[29] Lilienthal, *TVA Years*, pp. 711–713; Lilienthal, "Basis for Negotiation," October 13, 1933, *passim*.

[30] Lilienthal, *TVA Years*, p. 713.

[31] The following account of negotiations is from Lilienthal, "Basis for Negotiation," October 13, 1933; staff memorandum, "Relations with the Commonwealth and Southern Corporation," draft dated November 1938, pp. 1–15; Lilienthal to the board, memoranda dated October 19 and 20, November 1 and 15, December 12 and 13, 1933; Llewellyn Evans to Lilienthal, memoranda dated December 5 and 6, 1933, all in TVA Archives. See also Board Minutes, July 11, October 4, 13, 16, Nov. 27, and December 15, 1933; and *TVA Years*, pp. 711–715.

[32] The text of the contract is printed in *Hearings*, pp. 166–173. To alleviate unemployment, TVA put to work four six-hour shifts of men at Norris Dam, and the dam was completed within three years. Willkie therefore had less time under the umbrella of the January 4 truce than he expected to have.

[33] Norris to Lilienthal, telegram, August 18, 1933, Tray 69, box 4, Norris MSS.

Notes for Chapter 4, pp. 67–90

[1] TVA *Annual Report* (1934), pp. 24–26.

[2] *Hearings*, p. 168.

[3] Swidler to Lilienthal, office memorandum, March 29, 1934, TVA Archives. Swidler had worked in Lilienthal's office in Chicago. Subsequently he would become TVA's general counsel, then chairman of the Federal Power Commission and

the New York Public Service Commission.

[4] Lilienthal to Willkie, April 6, 1934, TVA Archives.

[5] U. S., House, Committee on Military Affairs, *Tennessee Valley Authority*, 74th Cong., 1st sess. (1935), p. 253; Willkie to Lilienthal, April 11, June 18, 1934; Lilienthal to Willkie, April 16, June 20 (two letters and one telegram), June 22 (telegram), 1934; "Relations with the Commonwealth and Southern Corporation," memorandum, November 1938, pp. 16–20, all in TVA Archives; Board Minutes, March 9 and 17, April 13, June 11, 15, and 30, July 17, August 6 and 9, November 19, 1934.

[6] *Hearings*, p. 168; James Lawrence Fly to Lilienthal, office memorandum, "Breaches of Contract of January 4, 1934, by power companies and Commonwealth and Southern Company," October 17, 1935; Lilienthal to Willkie, July 25, August 8 and 27, 1935; Willkie to Lilienthal, August 3 and 15, 1935; John C. Weadock (C & S counsel) to Lilienthal, August 29, 1935; Lilienthal to Weadock, August 31, 1935, all in TVA Archives; Lilienthal to Norris, "Memorandum of Facts," covering letter dated December 13, 1934, Tray 69, box 4, Norris MSS; Willkie to Marvin McIntyre, January 11, 1935, OF 293, Roosevelt MSS.

[7] Lilienthal to Roosevelt, August 9, 1934, OF 42, Roosevelt MSS; see also Chapter VII below.

[8] Roosevelt, *Public Papers and Addresses*, III, 461 (November 18, 1934). Almost every treatment of any kind dealing with the TVA power program contains some com-

ment on the yardstick. Of the plentiful literature on this subject the following were most helpful to the discussion here: Joseph S. Ransmeier, *The Tennessee Valley Authority: A Case Study in the Economics of Multiple Purpose Stream Planning* (Nashville: Vanderbilt University Press, 1942); Edward S. Mason, "Power Aspects of the Tennessee Valley Authority's Program," *Quarterly Journal of Economics*, L (May, 1936), 377–414; W. W. Cooper, "The Yardstick for Utility Regulation," *Journal of Political Economy*, LI (June, 1943), 258–262; Leland Olds, "Yardsticks and Birch Rods," *Harpers Magazine*, CLXXI (November, 1935), 648–659; Robert W. Harbeson, "The Power Program of the Tennessee Valley Authority," *Journal of Land & Public Utility Economics*, XII (February, 1936), 19–32; William I. Nichols, "Teaching Grandmother How to Spin: The TVA and the Private Utilities," *Harpers Magazine*, CLXXIII (July, 1936), 113–119; and Twentieth Century Fund, *Electric Power and Government Policy* (New York: Twentieth Century Fund, 1948), pp. 649–652.

[9] Minutes of the National Power Policy Committee meeting, January 27, 1937, Box 10, National Power Policy Committee Records (Record Group 48), National Archives (cited hereafter as NPPC Records).

[10] TVA press release, September 15, 1933. TVA Technical Library; Edward Falck to Lilienthal, February 26, 1934, office memorandum, TVA Archives.

[11] Lilienthal to Frankfurter, June 10, 1935, Box 71, Frankfurter MSS.

[12] TVA pamphlet, "How Cheap Electricity Pays Its Way," (Knoxville, 1937), pp. 4, 7, 29–30.

[13] Miller, *Kilowatts at Work*, p. 345; see also Henry I. Harriman, quoted in *Electrical World*, CIII (March 24, 1934), 451.

[14] The following discussion of the objective rate plan is from William F. Kennedy, *The Objective Rate Plan for Reducing the Price of Residential Electricity* (New York: Columbia University Press, 1937), *passim;* F. A. Newton, "The Commonwealth and Southern Objective Rate Plan," *Journal of Land and Public Utility Economics*, XI (May, 1935), 117–122; Clemens, *Economics and Public Utilities*, pp. 353–356; and *Fortune*, "Commonwealth and Southern," pp. 190, 195.

[15] Nichols, "Teaching Grandmother How to Spin," pp. 113–115.

[16] Quoted in Barnes, *Willkie*, p. 72; *Fortune*, "Commonwealth and Southern," pp. 187–188; Barnard, *Wendell Willkie*, pp. 94–96.

[17] George Fort Milton, "The Historical Background of Tennessee Electric Power Co.," undated memorandum, Box 89, Milton MSS.

[18] Jo. Conn Guild, address to Edison Electric Institute convention of 1935, printed in *Chattanooga Times*, June 5, 1935.

[19] *Ibid.; Fortune*, "Commonwealth and Southern," pp. 188, 190; Nichols, "Teaching Grandmother How to Spin," p. 114; Commonwealth and Southern Corporation, "Report to the Stockholders," 1935 and 1936, copies in the files of the Edison Electric Institute, New York, New York.

[20] Cooke to Ickes, April 6, 1934, Box 7, NPPC Records; Ickes to Roosevelt, July 3, 1934, OF 2575; Frank McNinch to Roosevelt, January 23, 1935, OF 235, both in Roosevelt MSS; Roosevelt, *Public Papers and Addresses*, III, 339–341; Philip J. Funigiello, "A Political and Legislative History of the Public Utility Holding Company Act of 1935," unpublished doctoral dissertation, New York University, 1966, Chapter III.

[21] Minutes of NPPC meetings July 18, August 29, December 20, 1934, and January 17, 1935, Box 10; Ickes, memorandum, December 20, 1934 Box 9; Wolfsohn to Benjamin Cohen, September 2, 1936, Box 6, all in NPPC Records; Wolfsohn to Ickes, memoranda, March 4 and December 31, 1936, OF 2575, Roosevelt MSS.

[22] This synopsis is from Funigiello, "A Political and Legislative History of the Public Utility Holding Company Act of 1935"; Michael E. Parrish, "Securities Regulation and the New Deal," unpublished doctoral dissertation, Yale University, 1968, Chapter V; Schlesinger, *The Politics of Upheaval*, pp. 302–324; Leuchtenburg, *Franklin D. Roosevelt and the New Deal*, pp. 154–157; Ellis W. Hawley, *The New Deal and the Problem of Monopoly: A Study in Economic Ambivalence* (Princeton: Princeton University Press, 1966), pp. 329–337.

[23] Lilienthal to Frankfurter, June 10, 1935, Box 71, Frankfurter MSS.

[24] Willkie, "A Discussion of the Wheeler-Rayburn Public Utility Bill," address over CBS radio, April 4, 1935, p. 5; Willkie, "Government's Relation to the Power Industry," address to 23rd annual meeting of

the Chamber of Commerce of the United States, May, 1935, pp. 6, 8, both in files of Edison Electric Institute. See also New York *Herald Tribune*, May 27, 1935; *New York Times*, March 15, April 2 and 21, May 2 and 22, 1935; Barnes, *Willkie*, pp. 79–95; and Willkie, "The Future of the Holding Company," *Journal of Land and Public Utility Economics*, XI (August, 1935), 234–239.

[25] Willkie, address before the Bond Club of New York, December 19, 1935, p. 9, files of Edison Electric Institute.

[26] James T. Patterson, *Congressional Conservatism and the New Deal: The Growth of the Conservative Coalition in Congress, 1933–1939* (Lexington: University of Kentucky Press, 1967), pp. 38–42.

[27] Schlesinger, *Coming of the New Deal*, pp. 282–288; Leuchtenburg, *Franklin D. Roosevelt and the New Deal*, pp. 133–134.

[28] Ickes, *Back to Work: The Story of PWA* (New York: Macmillan, 1935), pp. 136–137, 146; *New York Times*, November 1 and 3, 1933, December 21 and 26, 1934; Jack F. Isakoff, *The Public Works Administration* (Urbana: University of Illinois Press, 1938), pp. 109–111; J. Kerwin Williams, *Grants-in-Aid under the Public Works Administration* (New York: Columbia University Press, 1939), pp. 90–92, 112–113, 123, 154–158 (Williams writes that the policy of "bargaining" with power companies to reduce rates was sometimes done, but without the blessing of Ickes); Twentieth Century Fund, *Electric Power and Government Policy*, pp. 385–386, 395–399; Clark Foreman to Ickes, "Report to the Administrator on the

Status of Projects in the Power Division on December 31, 1935," February 3, 1936, Box 3, NPPC Records. Between 1933 and 1935, grants were restricted to amounts not exceeding 30 percent of the cost of labor and materials, the rest of the allotment being loans.

[29] Table 1, "PWA Allotments for Electric Power Projects as of November 1, 1936," Box 3, NPPC Records; Ickes to Norris, March 16, 1936, Tray 81, box 3, Norris MSS.

[30] This sketch of REA is based on Morris L. Cooke, "Early Days of Rural Electrification," *American Political Science Review, XLII* (June, 1948), 431–447; H. S. Person, "The Rural Electrification Administration in Perspective," *Agricultural History*, XXIV (April, 1950), 70–89; Harry Slattery, *Rural America Lights Up* (Washington, D. C.: National Home Library Foundation, 1940); Twentieth Century Fund, *Electric Power and Government Policy*, Chapter VIII; Leuchtenburg, *Franklin D. Roosevelt and the New Deal*, pp. 157–158; Schlesinger, *The Politics of Upheaval*, pp. 378–384; Clemens, *Economics and Public Utilities*, pp. 582–596.

[31] McCraw, *Morgan vs. Lilienthal*, Chapters III, V, and VI.

[32] On this aspect of the conservation movement see Hays, *Conservation and the Gospel of Efficiency*, Chapters I and XIII. Hays's description of Theodore Roosevelt's philosophy of conservation (pp. 266–271) could be applied with equal accuracy to Arthur Morgan's.

[33] "Excerpts from Report to the Stockholders of the Commonwealth & Southern Corporation," year ended

December 31, 1935, copy in OF 235, Roosevelt MSS.

34 Willkie to McIntyre, telegram, November 19, 1934, OF 42, Roosevelt MSS; Willkie to Frankfurter, March 26, 1936, Box 71, Frankfurter MSS. See also Chapter VI below.

Notes for Chapter 5, pp. 91–107

1 Sachs, memorandum for Roosevelt, July 24, 1936, Ben Grey to Roosevelt, March 20, 1936, both in OF 1983, Roosevelt MSS; Lilienthal, "Preliminary Memorandum of Conference with Alexander Sachs," March 26, 1936; Lilienthal, "Memorandum of Telephone Conversation — Mr. Alexander Sachs, April 3, 1936," p. 1, both in Lilienthal MSS. An earlier version of this chapter appeared in McCraw, *Morgan vs. Lilienthal*, pp. 67–80.

2 Martin G. Glaeser to Lilienthal, with attached memorandum "A Power Pool for the Southeast," June 25, 1936; Judson King, Bulletin No. 176 of the National Popular Government League, January 23, 1937, both in TVA Archives.

3 *Ibid.*; Basil Manly to Roosevelt, memorandum, September 29, 1936, OF 42, Roosevelt MSS.

4 Lilienthal to the board of directors, September 14, 1936, Lilienthal to Norris, September 14, 1936; James Lawrence Fly to Lilienthal, memorandum, "Validity of a Power Pool under Existing Legislation," September 24, 1936; Martin G. Glaeser to John B. Blandford, "Suggested Basis for Power Pool Discussions — Preliminary and Tentative," September 28, 1936, TVA Archives. See also Manly to Roosevelt, memorandum of September 29, 1936.

5 Willkie to Roosevelt, May 21, 1936, PPF 3111, Roosevelt MSS.

6 Lilienthal to the board of directors, memorandum, "An Appraisal of the Present Situation," February 20, 1936, pp. 1, 12–14, Lilienthal MSS.

7 Lilienthal, "Memorandum of Telephone Conversation Mr. Alexander Sachs;" Lilienthal to Glaeser and others, August 22, 1936, Glaeser MSS.

8 Lilienthal to A. E. Morgan and H. A. Morgan, "Conference with Wendell L. Willkie, Washington, May 8, 1936, 2:30 to 4:00 PM," May 26, 1936, printed in *Hearings*, pp. 864–865.

9 Lilienthal to Roosevelt, August 5, 1936, OF 42, Roosevelt MSS; Board Minutes, August 4, 1936.

10 Roosevelt to the board of directors, August 25, 1936, TVA Archives; Lilienthal, *TVA Years*, p. 64.

11 *Hearings*, p. 899. On the day of the conference, Harcourt Morgan was ill and unable to attend. Russell Leffingwell was out of the country, so Thomas Lamont of the Morgan firm attended in his place.

12 *New York Times*, September 20 and 30, October 18, 1936; *cf.* Washington *News*, October 1, 1936, *Babson's Reports*, December 14, 1936.

13 Wehle to Thomas Carr Powell, October 2, 1936, Box 40, Wehle MSS.

14 Lilienthal to La Follette, September 16, 1936; Lilienthal to Norris, September 14, 1936, both in Lilienthal MSS; Lilienthal to Norris, November 4, 1936, pp. 1–2, TVA Archives; Lilienthal to Frankfurter, August 20, 1936, Box 71, Frankfurter MSS.

15 *Hearings*, p. 15.

16 Lilienthal to Norris, November 4, 1936, pp. 4–9, 16–24; Glaeser to

Lilienthal, memorandum, October 13, 1936; Glaeser to Lilienthal, November 1, 1936; Glaeser to Lilienthal, "Memorandum of Analysis," December 8, 1936, all in TVA Archives.

[17] McCraw, *Morgan vs. Lilienthal*, pp. 72–74.

[18] Lilienthal to the board of directors, memorandum, "Regional Pooling," September 19, 1936; Lilienthal to Norris, November 4, 1936, pp. 9–10, both in TVA Archives; Manly to Roosevelt, September 29, 1936, OF 42, Roosevelt MSS.

[19] Lilienthal to Norris, November 4, 1936, pp. 11–15; Louis B. Wehle, *Hidden Threads of History: Wilson through Roosevelt* (New York: Macmillan, 1953), pp. 164–166; Sachs, memorandum on conference, "Perspective on Tasks Arising from President's Power Pool Conference with Special Reference to the TVA and Commonwealth and Southern," n.d. (October 1936), OF 1983, Roosevelt MSS.

[20] *Ibid.*

[21] James Lawrence Fly to Willkie, October 8 and 14, 1936; Fly to Wehle, October 9, 1936; Willkie to Fly, October 9 and 16, 1936, all in TVA Archives.

[22] *Ibid.;* Lilienthal to Norris, November 4, 1936, pp. 13–16.

[23] Ickes to Roosevelt, September 23, 1936; Roosevelt, memorandum for McIntyre, September 30, 1936, OF 42, Roosevelt MSS.

[24] Wehle, *op. cit.*, pp. 167–170; Willkie to Wehle, October 21, 1936; Lilienthal to Ickes, October 22, 1936; Morgan to Wehle, October 24, 1936; Wehle to Roosevelt, October 26, 1936, all in OF 42, Roosevelt MSS; Manly to Wehle, October 17, 1936, Box 40, Wehle MSS.

[25] Wehle, *op. cit.*, pp. 167–170; Manly to Wehle, October 17 and December 12, 1936; Wehle to Manly, October 19, 1936, all in Box 40, Wehle MSS; *New York Times*, October 18, 1936; Marguerite Owen (TVA's Washington representative) to Lilienthal, memorandum, October 26, 1936, TVA Archives; Ickes to Lilienthal, November 6, 1936, Lilienthal MSS; memorandum, "PWA Allotments for Electric Power Projects as of November 1, 1936," Box 3, NPPC Records. The allotments to Memphis and Jackson did not directly affect Willkie's companies, which did not operate in those cities. But Willkie was concerned on principle, and was directly threatened in other cities; see Chapter VII below.

[26] Norris to Roosevelt, November 13, 1936, Norris MSS; Moley, *After Seven Years*, pp. 353–354; Wehle, *Hidden Threads*, pp. 170–171.

[27] Wehle, *Hidden Threads*, pp. 171–175; McCraw, *Morgan vs. Lilienthal*, pp. 77–79.

[28] *Ibid.;* White House press release, January 26, 1937, OF 42, Roosevelt MSS. Lilienthal, McNinch, and Manly drafted FDR's letter scuttling the pool.

[29] *New York Herald-Tribune*, January 19, 1937.

[30] Manly to Norris, January 27, 1937, copy in OF 42, Roosevelt MSS.

[31] Sachs, memorandum for Roosevelt, "Notes on Social Defeatism in Current Anti-Power Pool Agitation and Urgency of Broader Conference for Effectuation of the President's Plan," January 16, 1937, pp. 1, 4, 9, OF 42, Roosevelt MSS.

[32] Lilienthal to Roosevelt, January 12, 1937, p. 4, OF 42, Roosevelt MSS.

Notes for Chapter 6, pp. 108–121

[1] Roosevelt to Norman Hapgood, February 24, 1936, PPF 2278, Roosevelt MSS; Forrest Allen to Judson King, April 11, 1938, Box 18, King MSS; the phrase "living in the courts" was used earlier by TVA's General Counsel, James Lawrence Fly: *Hearings*, p. 183.

[2] *New York Times*, November 26, 1934; *Hearings*, p. 4210; Morton Keller, *In Defense of Yesterday: James M. Beck and the Politics of Conservatism 1861–1936* (New York: Coward-McCann, 1958), pp. 263–264; C. H. Cramer, *Newton D. Baker: A Biography* (Cleveland and New York: World, 1961), pp. 262–264.

[3] Roosevelt to Baker, November 8, 1934, PPF 669, Roosevelt MSS.

[4] *New York Times*, December 18, 1934.

[5] Some of the TVA cases overlapped the PWA litigation, as the companies challenged both agencies in the same area, sometimes separately, sometimes together as co-conspirators. The data are from U. S., Federal Emergency Administration of Public Works, *Injunctions in Cases Involving Acts of Congress*, Senate Document 27, 75th Cong., 1st sess. (1937), pp. 5–27; and two other works with the same title reported to the same Congress: by the Securities and Exchange Commission (Senate Document 43), pp. 6–11, and the Tennessee Valley Authority (Senate Document 44), pp. 1–9. See also TVA legal department memorandum, "History of Injunction Suits Involv-

ing Tennessee Valley Authority," 1937, TVA Archives; and Federal Power Commission, *Restraining Orders and Injunctions Instituted against Public Electric Projects*, Senate Document 182, 74th Cong., 2nd sess. (1936).

[6] *Hearings*, pp. 174–183, 5000; *Congressional Record*, 75th Cong., 1st sess., pp. 2142, 2143. The summary which follows in the remainder of this chapter owes much to Joseph C. Swidler and Robert H. Marquis, "TVA in Court: A Study of TVA's Constitutional Litigation," *Iowa Law Review*, XXXII (January 1947), 296–326; and George D. Haimbaugh, Jr., "The TVA Cases: A Quarter Century Later," *Indiana Law Journal*, XLI (Winter, 1966), 197–227. The TVA *Annual Report* contains the texts of some decisions, as well as summaries of important litigation. See the reports for 1934 (p. 55), 1935 (pp. 58–60), 1936 (pp. 290–303), 1937 (pp. 366–368), 1938 (pp. 102–108, 405–416), and 1939 (pp. 108–114, 471–478).

[7] Richard P. Whiteley, "Report of the Federal Trade Commission in the Matter of Attacks, Both by Way of Propaganda and Court Action, against the Federal Government's Hydro-electric Program," unpublished memorandum, November 27, 1934, p. 3, OF 42, Roosevelt MSS; William Fitts, interview in Memphis State University Oral History Project (1969), hereafter cited as MSOH interview.

[8] Printed letter to preferred stockholders from "Protective Committee for Preferred Stockholders of Alabama Power Company," October 1, 1934, Files of Edison Electric Institute. During the New Deal,

stockholders' suits of various kinds occurred more frequently than in other periods.

[9] *Ashwander v. Tennessee Valley Authority,* 8 F. Supp. 893 (1934), 9 F. Supp. 965 (1935).

[10] *Ibid.;* Fitts, MSOH interview.

[11] *Tennessee Valley Authority v. Ashwander,* 78 F. (2d) 578 (1935).

[12] *Ashwander v. Tennessee Valley Authority,* 297 U. S. 288 (1936); Minton, "Supreme Court and the T.V.A.," address over nationwide NBC radio network, February 24, 1936, Files of Edison Electric Institute.

[13] *Ibid.;* Swidler and Marquis, "TVA in Court," p. 311.

[14] Lilienthal, *TVA Years,* p. 59.

[15] Willkie to Marvin McIntyre, telegram, November 19, 1934; Willkie to Roosevelt, November 19, 1934, both in OF 42, Roosevelt MSS; Willkie to Felix Frankfurter, March 26, 1936, Box 71, Frankfurter MSS; *Hearings,* pp. 4210, 4223–4224; Lilienthal to Norris, July 26, 1935, Tray 69, Box 4, Norris MSS; Edison Electric Institute *Bulletin,* III (August 1935), 297; *Wall Street Journal,* July 24, 1935; Birmingham *Post* (editorial), July 26, 1935.

[16] Lilienthal to Frankfurter, March 7, 1936, Box 71, Frankfurter MSS.

[17] 49 Stat. 1075; Roosevelt to TVA board, December 24, 1934; Arthur Morgan to Roosevelt, January 24, 1935, OF 42, Roosevelt MSS; Samuel McReynolds to George Fort Milton, June 14, 1935, in McReynolds files, Box 88 of Estes Kefauver MSS; *Congressional Record,* 74th Cong., 1st sess., pp. 7499, 11184; May, "Tennessee Valley Authority: Dangerous Socialistic Experiment," *Public Service Magazine,* LIX (July, 1935), 9–10. See also U.S., Congress, *Tennessee Valley Authority,* Hearings before the House Committee on Military Affairs, 74th Cong., 1st sess. (1935), *passim.* Congressman May became an even greater problem for the TVA when he ascended to the chairmanship of the House Military Affairs Committee.

[18] Swidler and Marquis, "TVA in Court," p. 313.

[19] Rankin to Norris, December 23, 1936, Tray 81, box 5, Norris MSS; *Tennessee Valley Authority v. Tennessee Electric Power Company,* 90 F. (2d) 885 (1937); TVA Washington Office memorandum, "19 Utilities' Litigation (A Chronology)," November 1, 1937, OF 42, Roosevelt MSS.

[20] William E. Leuchtenburg, "Franklin D. Roosevelt's Supreme Court 'Packing' Plan," in Harold M. Hollingsworth and William F. Holmes, eds., *Essays on the New Deal* (Austin: University of Texas Press, 1969); Leuchtenburg, "The Origins of Franklin D. Roosevelt's 'Court Packing' Plan," *The Supreme Court Review,* 1966, 347–400; Patterson, *Congressional Conservatism and the New Deal,* Chapter 3.

[21] Wehle, *Hidden Threads,* Chapter XVI; 50 Stat. 751; a draft of the bill, which is similar in several ways to the statute, is in a memorandum by two junior TVA lawyers, Herbert Marks and Bessie Margolin, "Anti-Injunction Legislation," January 14, 1937, TVA Archives (a partial copy is in Box 7 of the Herbert Marks MSS), Fly to Lilienthal, July 23, 1937; Fly to Senators McKellar, Black, and McCarran, and Congressman Summers, July 23, 1937, all in TVA Archives; Fitts, MSOH interview; Fly

to Norris, March 11, 1939, Tray 67, box 5, Norris MSS. See also Rankin to Norris, December 23, 1936, Tray 81, box 5, Norris MSS.

[22] *Tennessee Electric Power Company v. Tennessee Valley Authority,* 21 F. Supp. 947 (1938).

[23] *Tennessee Electric Power Company v. Tennessee Valley Authority,* 306 U.S. 118 (1939).

[24] Ickes to Norris, March 16, 1936, Tray 81, box 3, Norris MSS.

[25] *Alabama Power Company v. Ickes,* 302 U.S. 464 (1938).

[26] Federal Emergency Administration of Public Works, Release No. 3271 (PWA Press Section), January 3, 1938, copy in Tray 81, box 3, Norris MSS.

Notes for Chapter 7, pp. 122–139

[1] Lilienthal to Roosevelt, memorandum, July 21, 1937; Kenneth D. McKellar to J. D. Hasson, December 2, 1941, both in Box 337, McKellar MSS; Wilmon H. Droze, *High Dams and Slack Waters: TVA Rebuilds a River* (Baton Rouge: Louisiana State University Press, 1965), pp. 27–41; McKellar to Roosevelt, February 8, 1943, p. 3, OF 42, Roosevelt MSS.

[2] Lilienthal to Roosevelt, memorandum, July 21, 1937, pp. 4–5.

[3] *Hearings,* pp. 5293–5305; *Report of the Joint Committee,* pp. 164–168.

[4] Lilienthal, *TVA Years,* pp. 79–81; Lilienthal to Frankfurter, April 29 and July 27, 1934, Lilienthal MSS; the following are representative samples of Lilienthal's speeches (the quotation is from the first listed): address to Shelby County Young Democratic Club, broadcast over station WREC, Memphis, October 20, 1934; "Future of Industry in the Tennessee Valley Region," address to the Tennessee Valley Institute of the University of Chattanooga, April 11, 1934; "Five-Point Program for the Electrification of America," address to the Lawyers' Club, Atlanta, November 19, 1933; "Power Shortage and Business Recovery," address to Eight County Mass Meeting, Dickson, Tennessee, October 24, 1935, all in Lilienthal, "Speeches and Remarks," I, collected and bound by the TVA Technical Library, Knoxville.

[5] Coppock, "Government as Enterpriser-Competitor: The Case of the Electric Home and Farm Authority," 187–206; for a critical contemporary view of EHFA, see Ted Leitzell, "Uncle Sam, Peddler of Electric Gadgets," *New Outlook,* CLXIV (August, 1934), 50–53; Lilienthal to Frankfurter, April 29, 1934, Lilienthal MSS.

[6] R. L. Montgomery to Lilienthal, June 10, 1936, TVA Archives; Lilienthal to Frankfurter, April 29 and July 27, 1934, Lilienthal MSS.

[7] Fly to Lilienthal, memorandum, "State Legislation," March 17, 1936, TVA Archives; Fitts, MSOH interview; Victor C. Hobday, *Sparks at the Grass Roots: Municipal Distribution of TVA Electricity in Tennessee* (Knoxville: University of Tennessee Press, 1969), pp. 19–31, 172–218; Alexander T. Edelmann, "The T.V.A. and Inter-Governmental Relations," *American Political Science Review,* XXXVII (June, 1943), 455–469; Alexander T. Edelmann, "Kentucky Accepts T.V.A. Power," *Journal of Land and Public Utility Economics,* XVIII (November, 1942), 481–484.

[8] TVA staff memorandum, August,

1934, "History of the Knoxville Situation"; Lilienthal to Oscar Chapman, telegram and letter, November 28, 1933; Marguerite Owen to Lilienthal, telegram, December 5, 1933, all in TVA Archives; *New York Times,* November 28, 1933, January 23, 1934.

⁹ Lilienthal to Groesbeck, May 28 and June 12, 1934; Groesbeck to Lilienthal, June 8, 1934, all in TVA Archives; *New York Times,* February 26, June 14, 17, 20, 22, and July 13, 1934.

¹⁰ *New York Times,* July 18, 22, 31, September 6, October 27, November 1, 1934, January 9, March 28, 1935; March 8, 1936; October 12, 1937; February 25, May 10 and 20, August 25, September 1 and 3, 1938; Lilienthal to Roosevelt, December 11, 19, and 21, 1934; Roosevelt to Lilienthal, December 22, 1934, all in OF 42, Roosevelt MSS; Forrest Allen, memorandum, May 17, 1937; Lilienthal to George R. Dempster (Knoxville City Manager), August 13, 1937; TVA's Washington Office memorandum, February 24, 1938; W. W. Mynatt (Mayor of Knoxville) to Lilienthal, April 2, 1938, all in TVA Archives.

¹¹ Memphis *Commercial Appeal,* November 5, 1934.

¹² *Ibid.,* June 27, 1939; Crump to Norris, November 9, 1934, Tray 66, box 6, Norris MSS; M. O. Swanson, memorandum, "Memphis Situation," September 12, 1934; Joseph C. Swidler to the Files, "Report of Conference with Memphis Officials," April 7, 1936; Thomas Allen (Memphis power official) to Lilienthal, February 2 and June 30, 1938; Lilienthal to H. A. Morgan and J.

B. Blandford, memorandum, "City of Memphis Negotiations," July 18, 1938, all in TVA Archives.

¹³ Milton to Norris, September 27, 1935, Tray 69, box 8, Norris MSS; Milton to Roosevelt, telegram, March 12, 1935, OF 42, Roosevelt MSS.

¹⁴ *Hearings,* pp. 2600–2856 *passim;* Milton to Norris, March 14, 1935, Tray 69, box 8, Norris MSS. It was alleged that the power company's subsequent activities drove Milton and his paper, the *Chattanooga News,* out of business. This charge was partially true, but Milton's business failure was owing primarily to his defeat in a proxy fight for control of the newspaper.

¹⁵ Harold C. Fiske (Chairman of the Electric Power Board of Chattanooga) to TVA board, January 7, 1937, TVA Archives; the contract is printed in TVA's *Annual Report* (1938), pp. 167–180.

¹⁶ Fiske to Guild, February 18 and 20, 1936; Guild to Fiske, February 19, 1936; Fiske to Willkie, May 12, 1936; Willkie to Fiske, May 19, 1936; Milton to Roosevelt, May 23, 1936, all in OF 293, Roosevelt MSS.

¹⁷ Milton to McIntyre, October 27 and November 1, 1938, OF 42, Roosevelt MSS; L. J. Wilhoite to Willkie, July 7, 1938, p. 5, TVA Archives.

¹⁸ Lilienthal to La Follette, February 26, 1937; Helen Lilienthal, MS diary, August 21, 1936, both in Lilienthal MSS.

¹⁹ Morgan, address to Rotary Club of Columbus, Ohio, May 13, 1935, p. 14, in "Speeches and Remarks," II; Morgan, address over NBC radio, "What Is Public Business?" January 2, 1936, *ibid.;* Morgan, "Speeches

and Writings," I, section 5, p. 35, all in TVA Technical Library; Morgan to Lilienthal, June 25, 1936, Lilienthal MSS.

[20] Morgan wrote the following articles: "The Next Four Years in the T.V.A.," *New Republic*, LXXXIX (January 6, 1937), 290–294; statement in *New York Times*, January 17, 1937; "Public Ownership of Power," *Atlantic Monthly*, CLX (September, 1937), 339–346; "Yardstick—and What Else?" *Saturday Evening Post*, CCX (August 7, 1937), 5.

[21] On the feud's effect in the fight for appropriations, see McKellar to H. W. Booth, March 8, 1938, Box 337; and McKellar to Mora B. Fariss, January 4, 1938 (letter erroneously dated 1937), Box 8, both in McKellar MSS.

[22] McCraw, *Morgan vs. Lilienthal*, Chapter IX.

[23] The discussion which follows is based on documents in the TVA Archives, the most important being drafts by Julius Krug, Joseph Swidler, and Forrest Allen of memoranda entitled "Chronology: Commonwealth and Southern Relations, 1938," "Relations with the Commonwealth and Southern Corporation," and "Memorandum of the Positions of the Parties in the Recent Negotiations between TVA and the Commonwealth and Southern Corporation for the Purchase of Certain Utility Properties," all dated November 1938. See also Barnes, *Willkie*, Chapter 9; Barnard, *Wendell Willkie*, Chapter VI; *Hearings*, pp. 4262–4267, 4271–4277; and U.S., Congress, *Tennessee Valley Authority*, Hearings of a House Subcommittee of the Committee on Military Affairs, 76th Cong., 1st sess. (1939), pp. 2–16.

[24] L. J. Wilhoite, "Wilhoite at Long Last Reveals the Intimate Details of Purchase of Tennessee Power Co. from Willkie," *Chattanooga Times*, May 18, 1958.

[25] House Subcommittee, *Tennessee Valley Authority*, pp. 8–10; Barnes, *Willkie*, p. 147.

[26] Barnard, *Wendell Willkie*, p. 124; Barnes, *Willkie*, p. 148; Lilienthal, *TVA Years*, pp. 119–121.

[27] Barnard, *Wendell Willkie*, p. 124; the advertisement, entitled "Tonight at Midnight," appeared in all major New York papers on August 16, 1939, and also in, for example, the Cincinnati *Enquirer*, the Baltimore *Sun*, the Kansas City *Star*, the Chicago *Tribune*, and the Washington *Times-Herald*.

[28] Martin, *The Story of Electricity in Alabama*, p. 110.

[29] Local public power forces allied with TVA did not win referenda everywhere. They lost, for example, in Birmingham, Alabama, and Jackson, Mississippi. But in most cities, particularly those actually on the Tennessee River, TVA's allies won easily.

[30] *Hearings*, p. 4226; House Subcommittee, *Tennessee Valley Authority*, p. 253; House Military Affairs Committee, *Tennessee Valley Authority* (1935), p. 99; See also Harold L. Ickes, *The Lowering Clouds, 1939–1941* (New York: Simon and Schuster, 1954), p. 26; and Ickes, The Autobiography of a Curmudgeon (New York: Reynal & Hitchcock, 1943), pp. 295–296.

Notes for Chapter 8, pp. 140–161

[1] Harcourt Morgan, preface to projected (not completed) book, n.d. (c. 1950), p. 1, Harcourt Morgan MSS; Harcourt Morgan to Roosevelt, October 16, 1937, OF 42, Roosevelt MSS; Lilienthal, *TVA: Democracy on the March* (New York: Harper & Row, 1953, Twentieth Anniversary Edition), p. 125.

[2] TVA's agricultural program is analyzed in Norman I. Wengert, *Valley of Tomorrow: The TVA and Agriculture* (Knoxville: Bureau of Public Administration, University of Tennessee, 1952); and Philip Selznick, *TVA and the Grass Roots: A Study in the Sociology of Formal Organization* (Berkeley: University of California Press, 1949); see also TVA's own publications, such as "Soil — The Nation's Basic Heritage" (Knoxville: TVA, 1937), and "Fifty Inches of Rain" (Knoxville: TVA, 1939), Chapter III.

[3] Charles H. Houston and John P. Davis, "TVA: Lily-White Reconstruction," *The Crisis*, XLI (October, 1934), 291; Rollins L. Winslow, "An Alley in the Valley," *The Crisis*, XLIV (January, 1937), 12; Robert F. Jones to Lilienthal, n.d. (received June 20, 1938); John B. Blandford to Jones, July 8, 1938; Walter White to Lilienthal, October 2, 1935 and June 28, 1937; John P. Davis to Arthur Morgan, May 2, 1935, all in TVA Archives; *Hearings*, pp. 2347–2390; *cf.* James Rorty, "Black, White, and TVA," *The Crisis*, LIII (April 1946), 114.

[4] Selznick, *TVA and The Grass Roots*, pp. 238–242; *Hearings*, pp. 5427–5429; *Reports and Exhibits* of the Joint Committee Investigating the Tennessee Valley Authority (Senate Document 56, 76th Cong., 1st sess., Part 2), pp. 97–100.

[5] Hobday, *Sparks at the Grass Roots*, pp. 39–41.

[6] McKellar to Fred H. Human, December 12, 1941, Box 337, McKellar MSS; Arthur Morgan to Roosevelt, September 7, 1934, OF 42, Roosevelt MSS; Lilienthal to Frankfurter, June 10, 1935, Box 71, Frankfurter MSS; Lilienthal, memorandum, "Group Meeting on 'Planning,'" July 24, 1936, TVA Archives.

[7] Quoted in Herbert Agar review in *New Statesman and Nation*, XXVI (November 20, 1943), 339

[8] Commager, *The American Mind: An Interpretation of American Thought and Character since the 1880's* (New Haven: Yale University Press, 1950), p. 345.

[9] Unless otherwise noted, this summary of the activities of the Information Office is from William L. Sturdevant, "Review of Program and Policy of the Information Office," a TVA staff report, n.d. (1940), TVA Archives. For an overview of TVA's policies up to 1936, see Egbert S. Wengert, "The Public Relations of Selected Federal Administrative Agencies," unpublished doctoral dissertation, University of Wisconsin, 1936, pp. 189–254.

[10] Sturdevant, "Review of Program and Policy," pp. 11–16.

[11] *Ibid., passim;* TVA *Annual Report* (1936), p. 75; Harry C. Bauer, compiler, "An Indexed Bibliography of the Tennessee Valley Authority," mimeographed, 1936, with cumulative supplements, TVA Technical Library.

[12] Sturdevant, "Review of Program

and Policy," pp. 18–19, Appendix A, p. 2.

[13] Waldemar Kaempffert, "Power for the Abundant Life," *New York Times Magazine* (August 23, 1936), p. 21.

[14] Alabama Coal Companies, "Address of Wendell L. Willkie at Rotary Club, Birmingham, November 7, 1934," OF 284; Lilienthal to Roosevelt, October 16, 1934, OF 42; National Coal Association, "The Facts about the Billion Dollar Water Power Development of the Federal Government," August, 1934, OF 42; Milton H. Fies, form letter, n.d., OF 42, all in Roosevelt MSS; National Coal Association, series of five pamphlets, 1934–1935, copies in Files of Edison Electric Institute. When TVA in the 1950's and 1960's emerged as the nations's largest single purchaser of coal, these attacks from the coal industry in the earlier period seemed particularly ill-considered.

[15] Republican National Committee press release, October 14, 1936, Files of Edison Electric Institute; American Liberty League, "The TVA Amendments," Document 37, May 1935; American Liberty League, "Extending the TVA Idea," 1937 Bulletin Series, No. 7, June 21, 1937, copies in University of Kentucky Library, Lexington.

[16] Fly to Lilienthal, memorandum, "Alabama Power Company Advertisement," November 9, 1936, TVA Archives; examples of these ads may be found in Birmingham *Post,* March 16 and 17, 1936; Birmingham *News,* April 1 and 22, 1936; Montgomery *Advertiser,* December 28, 1936; Birmingham *Age-Herald,* March 16 and 18, April 13, 1936; H. J. Rosson to Lilienthal, January 21, 1938, TVA Archives.

[17] Willkie, "Government and the Public Utilities," address to a joint meeting of the Economic Club and the Harvard Business School Club, January 21, 1935, New York City, copy in Edison Electric Institute Files.

[18] This analysis is based on about fifteen of Willkie's magazine articles and the collection of about fifteen of his speeches in the Edison Electric Institute Files. A selection of fourteen pieces from Willkie's articles and speeches is printed in *This Is Wendell Willkie* (New York: Dodd, Mead, 1940). See also Chapters V and VI of Barnard, *Wendell Willkie,* and Chapters 6–9 of Barnes, *Willkie.*

[19] Lloyd M. Wells, "The Defense of 'Big Business' 1933–1953: A Study in the Development of an Ideology," unpublished doctoral dissertation, Princeton University, 1955, pp. 34–37, 45, 48, 53; Robert C. Gibson, "Political Attitudes of Selected American Business Periodicals: 1930–1955," unpublished doctoral dissertation, Ohio State University, 1961, pp. 32, 56–57.

[20] E. C. Carson to Lilienthal, May 18, 1936, TVA Archives; Samuel W. Levine to Howe, November 3, 1933, OF 42, Roosevelt MSS.

[21] Evans, Stillman & Co. to Howe, January 11, 1935, OF 284, Roosevelt MSS.

[22] Draft of reply to Walter K. Clarke, June 3, 1937, TVA Archives; Basil Manly, address to Institute of Public Affairs, University of Virginia, Charlottesville, July 15, 1935, OF 235, Roosevelt MSS.

[23] McNinch to Roosevelt, memorandum, November 16, 1937, OF 293, Roosevelt MSS; Lilienthal to Norris, November 26, 1937, Tray 69, box 4; Norris to Marshall McNeil, January 16, 1934, Tray 67, box 11, both in Norris MSS; Forrest Allen to Norris, memorandum, "The Power Trust Will Build, If—," March 17, 1939, TVA Archives; Ben W. Lewis, "The Government as Competitor: The Effect on Private Investment," *American Economic Review*, XXIX (June, 1939), 286–298.

[24] Arkwright to Roosevelt, September 9, 1936, OF 42, Roosevelt MSS. See also Ernest R. Abrams, "TVA and the Bond Market," *Public Utilities Fortnightly*, XIX (January 7, 1937), 24–28; Wright, *History of the Georgia Power Company*, p. 276; Willkie to Roosevelt, September 30, 1936 (not sent until January 1937), TVA Archives; Lawrence G. Dahl, "Some Comments on Public Utility Refunding Operations," *Journal of Land and Public Utility Economics*, XII (August 1936), 256–263.

[25] Philip J. Funigiello, "Kilowatts for Defense: The New Deal and the Coming of the Second World War," *Journal of American History*, LVI (December, 1969), 604–620; James C. Bonbright, *Public Utilities and the National Power Policies* (New York: Columbia University Press, 1940), p. 62; Judson King, "Re National Defense Power Program," memorandum, November 10, 1938, King MSS; Roosevelt to Norris, November 14, 1938, PPF 880; Leon Henderson to Roosevelt, November 19, 1940, OF 293, Ickes to Roosevelt, July 3 and 31, December 10, 1941, OF 2575, all in Roosevelt MSS.

[26] Keynes to Roosevelt, February 1, 1938, pp. 4–5, PPF 5235, Roosevelt MSS.

[27] Minutes of National Power Policy Committee meetings of January 19, 1937 and April 30, 1937; Cooke to "My colleagues on the President's Committee on National Power Policy," February 19, 1937, all in Box 10, NPPC Records.

[28] Roosevelt, *Public Papers and Addresses*, II, 123; Norris is quoted in William E. Leuchtenburg, "Roosevelt, Norris, and the 'Seven Little TVAs,'" *Journal of Politics*, XIV (August, 1952), 418; unless otherwise noted, this summary of the "seven sisters" proposal is taken from this article.

[29] Norris to Lilienthal, January 6, 1941, Tray 69, box 4, Norris MSS; Lilienthal, *TVA Years*, pp. 125–138.

[30] Daniels to Roosevelt, memorandum, March 18, 1944, OF 42, Roosevelt MSS; Wildavsky, "TVA and Power Politics," *American Political Science Review*, LV (September, 1961), 590.

[31] There is a book entitled *The Economic Impact of TVA* (John R. Moore, ed., Knoxville: University of Tennessee Press, 1967). A valuable and stimulating collection of eight essays, it does not begin to fulfill the promise of systematic analysis implicit in the title.

[32] Norris to Walter Locke, December 26, 1941, Tray 69, box 6, Norris MSS.

FOR
FURTHER READING

The Age of Roosevelt (Boston: Houghton Mifflin, 1957–1960), Arthur M. Schlesinger, Jr.'s massive eulogy of the New Deal, has so far reached three volumes, each an artistic triumph rich in detail: *The Crisis of the Old Order, 1919–1933* surveys the background, *The Coming of the New Deal* the first half of FDR's first term, and *The Politics of Upheaval* the second half. William E. Leuchtenburg, in his masterly *Franklin D. Roosevelt and the New Deal 1932–1940* (New York: Harper and Row, 1963), achieves better balance than Schlesinger, and provides a thorough bibliography that need not be duplicated here. Paul K. Conkin's interpretive essay, *The New Deal* (New York: Crowell, 1967), is critical, highly provocative, and in a very few words says almost as much about its subject as anything yet published. The tensions in New Deal economic policy, including power policy, are systematically analyzed in Ellis W. Hawley, *The New Deal and the Problem of Monopoly: A Study in Economic Ambivalence* (Princeton: Princeton University Press, 1966).

The Tennessee Valley Authority has inspired several dozen books and several thousand feature articles. Much of this literature is based on prior decisions to cheerlead or denounce. The TVA Technical Library, Knoxville, Tennessee, has kept careful track of practically all of it, and can furnish bibliographies to satisfy any student's appetite. The Authority's background is well recounted in Preston J. Hubbard, *Origins of the TVA: The Muscle Shoals Controversy* (Nashville: Vanderbilt University Press, 1961). The best general history of the TVA remains C. Herman Pritchett's *The Tennessee Valley Authority: A Study in Public Administration* (Chapel Hill: University of North Carolina Press, 1943). Also useful is Herman Finer's *The T.V.A.: Lessons for International Application* (Montreal: International Labor Office, 1944). David E. Lilienthal oversold his subject in *TVA: Democracy on the March* (New York: Harper and Row, Twentieth Anniversary Edition, 1953). A more balanced treatment by a board chairman is Gordon R. Clapp's *TVA: An Approach to the Development of a Region* (Chicago: University of Chicago Press, 1955). Two appealing but mostly uncritical studies by journalists are Willson Whitman, *God's Valley: People and Power along the Tennessee River* (New York: The Viking Press, 1939); and R.L. Duffus, *The Valley and Its People* (New York: Alfred A. Knopf, 1944). Useful specialized studies include Wilmon Henry Droze, *High Dams and Slack Waters: TVA Rebuilds a River* (Baton Rouge: Louisiana State University Press, 1965), a history of the navigation program; Joseph S. Ransmeier, *The Tennessee Valley Authority: A Case Study in the Economics of Multiple Purpose Stream Planning* (Nashville: Vanderbilt University Press, 1942); Philip Selznick, *TVA and the Grass Roots: A Study in the Sociology of Formal Organization* (Berkeley: University of California Press, 1949); Norman I. Wengert, *Valley of Tomorrow: The TVA and Agriculture* (Knoxville: Bureau of Public Administration, University of Tennessee, 1952); Thomas K. McCraw, *Morgan vs. Lilienthal: The Feud Within the TVA* (Chicago: Loyola University Press, 1970); Victor C. Hobday, *Sparks at the Grass Roots: Municipal Distribution of TVA Electricity in Tennessee* (Knoxville: University of Tennessee Press, 1969); John R. Moore (ed.), *The Economic Impact of TVA* (Knoxville: University of Tennessee Press, 1967); J.H. Kyle, *The Building of TVA: An Illustrated History* (Baton Rouge:

Louisiana State University Press, 1958); Harry L. Case, *Personnel Policy in a Public Agency: The TVA Experience* (New York: Harper and Brothers, 1955); and Aaron Wildavsky, *Dixon-Yates: A Study in Power Politics* (New Haven: Yale University Press, 1962).

The most comprehensive treatment of the power issue is the ponderous volume by the staff of the Twentieth Century Fund, *Electric Power and Government Policy: A Survey of the Relations between the Government and the Electric Power Industry* (New York: Twentieth Century Fund, 1948). An excellent brief analysis is James C. Bonbright, *Public Utilities and the National Power Policies* (New York: Columbia University Press, 1940). Useful information about the industry appears throughout Forrest McDonald's *Insull* (Chicago: University of Chicago Press, 1962), and his *Let There Be Light: The Electric Industry in Wisconsin 1881–1955* (Madison: American History Research Center, 1957). Of several company histories now available, the best by far is Raymond C. Miller's *Kilowatts at Work: A History of the Detroit Edison Company* (Detroit: Wayne State University Press, 1957). In 1935 the Commonwealth and Southern Corporation issued an 89-page "Outline of History and Development" (New York: privately printed), which remains the best single source on that company. Recent partisan works on the utility issue include Edwin Vennard, *Government in the Power Business* (New York: McGraw-Hill, 1968), a denunciation of public power; and Lee Metcalf and Vic Reinemer, *Overcharge* (New York: David McKay, 1967), a muckraking of private utility companies. A striking contemporary treatment of the power issue in the 1930s is Arthur Arent's "Power—A Living Newspaper," in *Federal Theatre Plays* (New York: Random House, 1938).

One fruitful approach to the utility question is through trade periodicals, such as *Public Utilities Fortnightly, Electrical World, Public Service Magazine,* and the Edison Electric Institute *Bulletin,* all of which usually offered the perspective of the private power tradition. *Public Ownership* presented the public tradition's viewpoint. Greater balance emerged in the scholarly *Journal of Land and Public Utility Economics,* and in several impressive articles in *Fortune,* notably in the issues of May 1935, May 1937, and February 1938.

Some of the leading figures in the power fight have been served well by biographers, others poorly, and many not at all. Chief among dozens of useful studies of Roosevelt are Frank Freidel's three superb volumes, *Franklin D. Roosevelt: The Apprenticeship,* ... *The Ordeal,* and ... *The Triumph* (Boston: Little, Brown, 1952–1956), which take Roosevelt through the 1932 election. James MacGregor Burns covers the New Deal in *Roosevelt: The Lion and the Fox* (New York: Harcourt, Brace, 1956), and the war years in *Roosevelt: The Soldier of Freedom* (New York: Harcourt Brace Jovanovich, 1970). Daniel R. Fusfeld ably analyzes *The Economic Thought of Franklin D. Roosevelt and the Origins of the New Deal* (New York: Columbia University Press, 1956), and Bernard Bellush illuminates *Franklin D. Roosevelt as Governor of New York* (New York: Columbia University Press, 1955). Two excellent books by members of FDR's official family are Rexford G. Tugwell, *The Democratic Roosevelt: A Biography of Franklin D. Roosevelt* (Garden City, New York: Doubleday, 1957), and Frances Perkins, *The Roosevelt I Knew* (New York: The Viking Press, 1946). Samuel I. Rosenman's compilation of *The Public Papers and Addresses of Franklin D. Roosevelt* (New York, 1938–1950; Vols. 1–5 published by Random House, 6–9 by Macmillan, and 10–13 by Harper and Brothers) is invaluable, and the same is true of Elliott Roosevelt (ed., with the assistance of Joseph P. Lash), *F.D.R.: His Personal Letters, 1928–1945* (two vols., New York: Duell, Sloan and Pearce, 1950). Richard Lowitt's admirable biography of Norris has so far examined *George W. Norris: The Making of a Progressive, 1861–1912* (Syracuse: Syracuse University

Press, 1963). Norman L. Zucker's *George W. Norris: Gentle Knight of American Democracy* (Urbana: University of Illinois Press, 1966), is brief and perceptive. Still useful is Alfred Lief's *Democracy's Norris: The Biography of a Lonely Crusade* (New York: Stackpole Sons, 1939). Norris told his own story in *Fighting Liberal: The Autobiography of George W. Norris* (New York: Macmillan, 1945). The best biographies of Willkie are Ellsworth Barnard's scholarly *Wendell Willkie...Fighter for Freedom* (Marquette: Northern Michigan University Press, 1966), and Joseph Barnes's *Willkie: The Events He Was Part Of — The Ideas He Fought For* (New York: Simon and Schuster, 1952). Mary Earhart Dillon's *Wendell Willkie, 1892–1944* (Philadelphia: J.B. Lippincott, 1952), is well written but slightly inaccurate. Muriel Rukeyser's book on Willkie, *One Life* (New York: Simon and Schuster, 1957), is an often fascinating literary piece in prose and poetry. Willkie's own *This is Wendell Willkie* (New York: Dodd, Mead, 1940) provides a sampler of speeches and articles. David E. Lilienthal emerges best from his own writings, especially his *Journals*, which have now reached four volumes: *The TVA Years, 1939–1945, The Atomic Energy Years, 1945–1950, The Venturesome Years, 1950–1955*, and *The Road to Change, 1955–1959* (New York: Harper and Row, 1964–1969). The only biography of a TVA director so far published is Willson Whitman's superficial, adulatory *David Lilienthal: Public Servant in a Power Age* (New York: Henry Holt, 1948). The career of one figure important in the power fight is examined in Kenneth E. Trombley's *The Life and Times of a Happy Liberal: A Biography of Morris Llewellyn Cooke* (New York: Harper and Brothers, 1954).

MANUSCRIPT COLLECTIONS AND OTHER UNPUBLISHED SOURCES

The most important source for this book was the Tennessee Valley Authority Archives (especially the Administrative Files), Knoxville, Tennessee. The TVA Technical Library maintains a voluminous clipping file which facilitates the work of any researcher.

Also essential were the Franklin D. Roosevelt Papers, Franklin D. Roosevelt Library, Hyde Park, New York (FDRL); the George W. Norris Papers, Manuscript Division, Library of Congress (LC); the Arthur E. Morgan Papers, Olive Kettering Library, Antioch College, Yellow Springs, Ohio; and the David E. Lilienthal Papers, Harvey Firestone Memorial Library, Princeton University, Princeton, New Jersey.

The following collections were quite helpful: the Judson King, Felix Frankfurter, and George Fort Milton Papers, all in LC; the National Power Policy Committee Records, National Archives; the Files of the Edison Electric Institute, New York, New York; the Memphis State University Oral History Research Office and the Kenneth D. McKellar Papers, Memphis Public Library, both in Memphis, Tennessee; and the Harcourt A. Morgan and Martin G. Glaeser Papers, both privately held.

Marginally useful were the Morris L. Cooke, Louis B. Wehle, Herbert Marks, John M. Carmody, and Leland Olds Papers, all in FDRL; the Julius A. Krug Papers, LC; and the Papers of Harry A. Curtis, James P. Pope, and Estes Kefauver (which also contain the TVA files of Congressman Samuel D. McReynolds), all in the University of Tennessee Library, Knoxville, Tennessee.

The records of the Commonwealth and Southern Corporation are not open to researchers. I was granted access to the privately held Wendell L. Willkie Papers too late to use them for this book. According to Ellsworth Barnard, the biographer who used this material, Willkie's correspondence as president of Commonwealth and Southern is absent from the collection, though listed on its inventory.

INDEX